# A Catholic Catechism of Social Questions
by Rev. J. O'Kane

with a preface by
Right Rev. Mgr. H. Forbes, D.D,
The Catholic Social Guild Oxford

NIHIL OBSTAT
Henricus Canonicus Forbes,
Censor Deputatus.

† IMPRIMATUR
Gulielmus Canonicas Daly,
Vicarius Generalis.

JUNE 17, 1935.

First Edition, February, 1936
Second Edition, April, 1936
Reprinted, July, 1936; November, 1936,
April, 1937; August, 1937; February, 1938; September, 1938;
June, 1939; October, 1941; August, 1942; December, 1942;
July, 1944; June, 1945; April, 1946; November, 1946; August, 1947;
May, 1948; March, 1949; February, 1950; June, 1951; May, 1952;
March, 1953; May, 1954; February, 1955; March, 1956

2011 EDITION NEWLY TYPESET AND PUBLISHED BY

LORETO PUBLICATIONS
P. O. BOX 603
FITZWILLIAM, NEW HAMPSHIRE 03447
603-239-6671    WWW.LORETOPUBS.ORG

ALL RIGHTS RESERVED
ISBN 1-930278-0-98
PRINTED AND BOUND IN THE UNITED STATES

# PART I
## CHAPTER

| | |
|---|---|
| 1. INTRODUCTION | 1 |
| 2. THE WORLD INTO WHICH MAN IS BORN | 3 |
| 3. MAN-HIS NATURE, ORIGIN, PURPOSE, AND DESTINY | 4 |
| 4. THE FALL OF MAN | 8 |
| 5. MAN-REDEEMED BY JESUS CHRIST | 10 |
| 6. LAW | 12 |
|    SECTION 1: THE NATURAL LAW | 12 |
|    SECTION 2: DIVINE POSITIVE LAW | 16 |

# PART II
## CHAPTER

| | |
|---|---|
| 7. LIFE | 21 |
|    SECTION 1: REGARDING ONE'S OWN LIFE | 21 |
|    SECTION 2: REGARDING THE LIFE OF OTHERS | 24 |
| 8. EDUCATION | 26 |
| 9. MARRIAGE | 33 |
| 10. THE RIGHT TO PRIVATE PROPERTY | 43 |
| 11. THE RIGHT TO A LIVING WAGE | 51 |
| 12. THE INDIVIDUAL | 60 |
| 13. THE FAMILY AND THE HOME | 66 |
| 14. THE STATE | 70 |
| 15. THE CATHOLIC AND POLITICS | 76 |

PREFACE

Seeing that the defense of faith and morals and perhaps in a greater degree their propagation, are becoming more and more the work of the laity, what could be more opportune than the publication of this little book? Here, indeed, is the primer of the lay apostolate.

A priest working on the mission in an industrial area meets, on a small scale, everything that is evil in the big, big world. Hence it is that Father O' Kane in writing a catechism to meet the needs of his own people has produced a work that will be useful everywhere and to all.

The Catholic Social Guild was quick to see this, and deserves well of the community for having made it accessible to all.

To face the world with safety, Catholics must have knowledge and character—they must know their religion and live it. The revolt from authority in religion, which began in the sixteenth century, has now become a revolt from authority in conduct as well.

Outside the Catholic Church there are very few nowadays who give a thought to what is God's will—the point of view of faith—God's plan. To the Catholic heart this indifference brings great sadness, but there is something sadder still; the world is actually in revolt against God, it is attacking God, blaspheming the good God, and doing its very best to banish God, his Christ, and Christ's Church from among men. And the fiercest of the fight is around the souls of our little ones, for they know that they have won the war if they can blot out the image of God from the souls of his children.

A CATHOLIC CATECHISM OF SOCIAL QUESTIONS

There are many religious bodies that call themselves Christian, but not one of them can withstand this anti-God campaign, except the Catholic Church—the true Church of Christ, built upon the Rock, St. Peter, and against which the gates of hell shall never prevail. Every loyal son of the Church therefore is bound to do what he can to be ready and to prepare others to fight successfully the battles of Christ the King. Here is his textbook, and we wish it Godspeed.

H. Forbes, St. Peter's College, Bearsden.
Feast of St. Joseph, March 19, 1936.

AUTHOR'S NOTE

In view of the nature of this book, it was deemed inadvisable to burden the text with references and footnotes. However, a list of books has been included for two reasons: firstly, to acknowledge the help which the authors and publishers have afforded in compiling the present statement; and, secondly, to enable the reader to pursue a wider study and form a better acquaintance with the questions under review.

*Rerum novarum* - Leo XIII
*Quadragesimo anno* - Pius XI
*Divini redemptoris* - Pius XI
*Casti connubii* - Pius XI
*Divini illus magistri* - Pius XI
*Women's Duties in Social and Political Life* - Pius XII

# PART I

## CHAPTER I
## INTRODUCTION

**QUESTION 1:** Has a Catholic any safe guide to social problems?
**ANSWER:** Every Catholic has safe and sound guidance in all the problems of life in the example and teaching of Jesus Christ.
*Catholic: A Christian is one who professes to be a follower of Christ. A Catholic is a Christian who has been baptized into the true faith of the Catholic Church.*

**QUESTION 2:** Did Jesus Christ claim to be a social leader and teacher of men?
**ANSWER:** Jesus Christ claimed to be not only the leader of men, but he claimed and proved himself to be the Son of God.
*Leader of men: "I am the way, the truth, and the life." (Jn. 14:6.)*
*Son of God: Proved by his fulfillment of prophecies, by his miracles, and especially by his Resurrection.*

**QUESTION 3:** What follows from the fact that Jesus Christ was God?
**ANSWER:** It follows from the divinity of Jesus Christ that his teaching is the Word of God, and all his doctrine is divine.

**QUESTION 4:** Did Jesus Christ give us any definite program for guidance on social questions?
**ANSWER:** Jesus Christ did not give us any cut-and-dry program on these problems, but he gave us the guiding principles by which alone these problems may be solved.
*Guiding principles: Rules to follow regarding man himself, regarding his relations with other men, and with God.*

**QUESTION 5:** Where are to be found those guiding principles laid down by Jesus Christ?
**ANSWER:** These guiding principles are to be found in the teaching of the one, holy, Catholic, and Apostolic Church which he established.

# A CATHOLIC CATECHISM OF SOCIAL QUESTIONS

*One, holy, Catholic, and Apostolic Church: Christ founded one Church, and gave her certain identification marks by which all men might easily recognize her as his Church. The Catholic Church alone possesses these marks.*

QUESTION 6: **What authority does the Catholic Church claim for her teaching?**
ANSWER: The Catholic Church claims the same authority as Jesus Christ had.
*Same authority: "As the Father hath sent me, I also send you." (Jn. 20:21.) "He that heareth you, heareth me." (Lk. 10:16.) "Go ye and teach all nations.... Behold I am with you all days." (Mt. 28:19, 20.)*

QUESTION 7: **Can the Catholic Church err in what she teaches?**
ANSWER: The Catholic Church cannot err in her teaching on questions of faith and morals.
*Cannot err: Christ promised that the gates of hell would not prevail against his Church; and that he himself would be with her all days, even to the end of the world. (Mt. 16:18; Mt. 28:20.)*

QUESTION 8: **Since the Church was established for the saving of souls, why should she concern herself with social conditions and problems?**
ANSWER: Because she must deal with man as he is, the whole man, in his surroundings, and in all his relations of life.
*Man as he is: of a complex nature—body and soul. Man is not isolated, but is a member of a family and of a community.*

QUESTION 9: **Are Catholics bound to follow and obey the Church on all social questions?**
ANSWER: Catholics are bound to obey the Church on such questions as involve principles of faith or morals, because she is our infallible guide on these principles.
*Infallible guide: One who cannot lead us astray.*

QUESTION 10: **Are all men bound to accept the teaching and obey the commands of Christ and his Church?**
ANSWER: Not only are all individuals bound to obey Christ and his Church on matters concerning faith or morals, but all civil corporations, governments, and states are likewise bound.

QUESTION 11: What sanction does Christ give to the teaching and commands of his Church?
ANSWER: The sanction which the Church holds for her teaching and commands on matters concerning faith and morals is the eternal sanction of heaven or hell.
*Sanction: "He that heareth you, heareth me; he that despiseth you, despiseth me." (Lk. 10:16.) "It is appointed unto men once to die, and after this, the judgment." (Heb. 9:27.)*

CHAPTER 2

THE WORLD INTO WHICH MAN IS BORN AND IN WHICH HE LIVES

QUESTION 12: What does the Catholic Church teach with regard to the origin of the world?
ANSWER: The Catholic Church teaches that God created the whole world out of nothing.
*Whole world: Sun, moon, planets. He created the first living things from which all existing living things are descended. Lastly he created man.*
*Out of nothing: They had no previous existence.*

QUESTION 13: For what purpose did God create the whole world?
ANSWER: The Catholic Church teaches that God's primary purpose in creating the world and everything in it was his own external glory.
*Primary purpose: First and principal reason for his act.*
*God's external glory: God is infinitely perfect, and cannot increase his perfection; but God can and did communicate some of his perfection to his creatures. These creatures reflect God's perfections, e.g., his wisdom, goodness, etc., and thus give external glory to God.*

QUESTION 14: Besides this primary purpose, did God create the world for any other purpose?
ANSWER: The Church teaches that the secondary purpose of God's creation is the happiness of his rational creatures.
*Rational creatures: Angels and men.*

A CATHOLIC CATECHISM OF SOCIAL QUESTIONS

CHAPTER 3

MAN: HIS NATURE, ORIGIN, PURPOSE, AND DESTINY

QUESTION 15: What position or dignity has man among the things of creation?
ANSWER: Man is the noblest creature of the visible world, and derives his dignity from the fact that he is made to the image and likeness of God.
*Noblest creature: In creating sun, moon, stars, planets, and animals, God merely said, "Let them be!" When he came to the creation of man God said, "Let Us make man to our own image and likeness." God also gave man dominion over the other creatures.*
*Image and likeness: Chiefly in the soul, because of its nature and qualities.*

QUESTION 16: What does the Church teach regarding the nature of man?
ANSWER: The Catholic Church teaches that man is composed of two constituents—body and soul, not merely existing side by side, but so united as to give unity of nature.

QUESTION 17: Which is the more important, body or soul?
ANSWER: The Church teaches that the soul is the more important, because it is the principle of all life in man; moreover, it is spiritual and immortal.
*All life in man: The soul is the principle of vegetative life (by reason of which a man grows), of sensitive life (by reason of which a man feels), and of intellectual life (by reason of which a man thinks, understands, and chooses freely).*
*Spiritual: It is not made up of parts, distinct and separable. It is utterly different from matter.*
*Immortal: Cannot die. The soul, once created, demands continued existence forever.*

QUESTION 18: What does the Church teach regarding the origin of man's soul?
ANSWER: The Catholic Church teaches that God directly created the soul of Adam, and that God directly creates every human soul.
*Directly created: God immediately and by a special act above the powers of nature produces the soul.*

QUESTION 19: **What does the Church teach with regard to the origin of the human body?**

ANSWER: The more common view of theologians has always held the traditional and obvious interpretation of Sacred Scripture (Genesis 2:8), namely that the body of Adam was made by God directly and by a special act.
*Genesis 2:8: "And the Lord God formed man of the slime of the earth, and breathed into his face the breath of life."*

QUESTION 20: **Does not the teaching of the Church contradict the conclusions of science which go to show that the human body is evolved from the lower animals?**
ANSWER: Truth cannot contradict truth. God is the author of reason, and author of his own teaching, and cannot contradict himself. Hence the truths of real science must harmonize with his own revealed teaching.
*Real science: We must beware of "popularizers of science" who with vivid imagination and facile pen describe as facts what are merely suppositions. That which has never been demonstrated cannot be admitted as a conclusion of science.*

QUESTION 21: **Are all men descended from Adam and Eve?**
ANSWER: The Church teaches that the whole human race is descended from Adam and Eve.
*Whole human race: It follows from the above answer that the whole human race is one, and that all human beings come from the same origin, with the same laws in their nature.*

QUESTION 22: **Why did God create man?**
ANSWER: It is the teaching of the Church that man was created primarily for God's external glory.
*God's external glory: Man is the most perfect of visible creatures, and reflects more than others the excellence of God; moreover, being rational, he can know and praise the excellence of his Creator.*

QUESTION 23: **Was this the only reason why God created man?**
ANSWER: The Church teaches that besides creating man for his own glory, God created man to make him a sharer of his happiness in heaven.

*Happiness in heaven: God could have given man a destiny of merely natural happiness, in keeping with his nature and faculties; but God did not in point of fact give man such a destiny. God gave man a destiny infinitely superior to any natural destiny, namely the happiness of heaven.*

QUESTION 24: Of what does the happiness of heaven consist?
ANSWER: The Church teaches that the happiness of heaven, for which man is destined, is the possession of God.
*Possession of God: That is, the face-to-face vision of God, or, as it is called, the Beatific Vision, with the love of it and the joy of possessing it which results from that vision.*

QUESTION 25: Has man by reason of his nature any claim to this destiny?
ANSWER: The Church teaches that this destiny of man is entirely above the claims of man, and is a free gift of God.
*Above claims of man: It is the definite and complete adoption of men as children of God. No one has a claim to be adopted.*

QUESTION 26: Is it within the power of man's unaided nature to reach this destiny?
ANSWER: The Church teaches that this destiny of man is beyond the reach of man's unaided natural powers, and is therefore entirely supernatural.
*Beyond man's natural powers: (a) Man could not even know of such a destiny unless God revealed it to him; (b) Man needs new extra powers if he is to attain an end utterly beyond the powers of his human nature.*

QUESTION 27: Since this destiny was beyond man's natural powers, did God bestow on man what was necessary to reach it?
ANSWER: The Church teaches that in preparation for, and in keeping with, this supernatural destiny God gave man the gift of supernatural life.
*Supernatural life: A life above nature, whereby even in this life his soul was "supernaturalized", capable of a relationship with God altogether higher and holier than anything that could spring from man's merely natural endowments.*

QUESTION 28: What was the source of this supernatural life?
ANSWER: The source and principle of this supernatural life which was given to man was God's sanctifying grace.

*Sanctifying grace: The most precious of God's gifts, which made our first parents "participators in the divine Nature," so that after their probation they were to pass from this world and dwell with God as children with their father. With this sanctifying grace man received the infused virtues of Faith, Hope, and Charity, enabling him to know, love, and serve God in a supernatural manner.*

QUESTION 29: Did God give man any other gifts with the gift of sanctifying grace?
ANSWER: The Church teaches that God gave man praeternatural gifts of integrity and immortality as suitable complements of his sanctifying grace.
*Praeternatural: Not due to nature, yet perfecting nature. They are not, however, "supernaturalizing" gifts.*
*Integrity: The interior harmony of the elements of his nature—his body and senses subordinate to mind and will, and these subjected by grace to God.*
*Immortality: Freedom from death.*

QUESTION 30: Were these gifts of sanctifying grace, integrity, and immortality, given to our first father, Adam, unconditionally?
ANSWER: The Church teaches that God gave these gifts to Adam to be held by Adam on condition that he observed the command imposed on him by God.
*Condition: "God made an everlasting covenant with them, and he showed them his justice and his judgments." (Eccl. 17:10.) "In what day soever thou shalt eat of it (the tree of knowledge), thou shalt die the death." (Genesis 2:17.)*

QUESTION 31: Was man free to retain the supernatural life or reject it?
ANSWER: The Church teaches that God gave man the necessary knowledge of the purpose of life (supernatural destiny), and the means to attain it (supernatural life of grace), and of the law to be obeyed, but God left man perfectly free to obey or disobey.
*Perfectly free: God does not force even his best gifts on man's free will. Sanctifying grace left man's will its natural prerogative of freedom. This free will, while, giving man his dignity among creatures, may also be the source of his downfall. And so it happened.*

QUESTION 32: Did God intend that all men should enjoy these supernatural and praeternatural gifts?

ANSWER: The Church teaches that God intended all men to receive the same gifts that adorned our first parents; such was God's scheme for all men, and God on his part left nothing undone to assure its happy fulfillment.

*God's scheme: The fact that men are born into the world in a condition which God never intended is the result of man's free will, which wrecked God's scheme, as we shall see.*

CHAPTER 4
THE FALL OF MAN

QUESTION 33: **Did man retain the supernatural life?**
ANSWER: The Church teaches that Adam sinned grievously—that is, rebelled against God—and thereby lost the supernatural life.
*Sinned grievously: The gravity of the offence was impressed on Adam by God when he declared the punishment which it would entail.*
*Lost supernatural life: This life cannot exist without love of God, and love of God cannot be where there is rebellion against him.*

QUESTION 34: **Did this original sin of Adam affect the rest of mankind?**
ANSWER: The Church teaches that in the fall of Adam (who was the head of the human race, in whom all men were incorporated) the whole human race fell, and lost the supernatural life of grace.
*Head of human race: Adam represented all men. He was the human race.*
*Whole human race fell: In Adam all died. (Rom. 5.) Loss of life means death; and therefore, supernaturally, men are born dead.*

QUESTION 35: **Does original sin in man mean merely absence of supernatural life?**
ANSWER: The Church teaches that original sin is not mere absence of supernatural life, but the deprivation of supernatural life.
*Deprivation: Absence of what we ought to have; which absence is due to rejection by Adam as head of the race.*

QUESTION 36: What is the chief consequence of original sin as it affects the human race?
ANSWER: The Church teaches that the chief consequence of original sin is that everyone born of Adam in the ordinary course of nature—the Blessed Virgin alone excepted—is from the first moment of existence in the state of sin.

*Blessed Virgin alone excepted: Who, by a singular privilege, and through the merits of her divine Son, was conceived without guilt or stain of original sin.*

*State of sin: The child begins its life in a condition brought about by the sin of Adam and contrary to the will of God, and therefore in a state hostile to God.*

QUESTION 37: Did man lose the other gifts which God gave to man as complements of the supernatural life?
ANSWER: The Church teaches that by original sin Adam lost to himself and to the whole race the praeternatural gifts of integrity and immortality.

*Lost integrity: Resulting in inordinate inclination to evil.*
*Lost immortality: "It is appointed unto man once to die." (Heb, 9:27.)*

QUESTION 38: Has man's human nature lost anything or suffered through original sin?
ANSWER: The Church teaches that original sin did not change human nature nor corrupt it, but it lost the added magnificence and vigor which it enjoyed through being elevated and supernaturalized by grace; and in that sense has suffered.

*Human nature not changed: There is still union of soul and body, with all their faculties, and everything due to nature.*
*Lost magnificence and vigor: Lost these by falling from the supernatural state. Human nature was then thrown back on itself and on its own powers, and thus suffered.*

QUESTION 39: In what position did man find himself as a consequence of the fall from grace?
ANSWER: The Church teaches that in consequence of original sin man was left with: (a) Human nature; (b) a supernatural destiny; and (c) no means by which he could reach it.

*No means: He lost the supernatural life, and therefore lost the possibility of reaching his destiny. Heaven was thus closed to the human race. Man could do nothing of himself to reopen it.*

A CATHOLIC CATECHISM OF SOCIAL QUESTIONS

CHAPTER 5
MAN: REDEEMED BY JESUS CHRIST

QUESTION 40: **Did God leave man in his hopeless position?**
ANSWER: No. God, out of his goodness and mercy, held out to man the hope of pardon, and promise of a Redeemer, who would do for man what man could not do for himself.

QUESTION 41: **Did this Redeemer come?**
ANSWER: The Church teaches that this Redeemer came in the person of God the Son, made man for us.
*God the Son made man:* Being God, he took to himself a complete human nature like ours, and made it his own. He is therefore One Person, God, with two natures—divine and human.

QUESTION 42: **What did Jesus Christ accomplish for man?**
ANSWER: The Church teaches that Jesus Christ, true God and true man, freely offered his suffering and death to his heavenly Father in atonement for the sins of men, satisfying the justice of his Father, and reconciling the human race to God.
*Freely offered:* "No man taketh away my life from me, but I lay it down of myself." (Jn. 10:18.)
*In atonement for sin:* Sin is an offence of infinite malice. God's justice demands infinite satisfaction. Moreover, a human act of rebellion requires a human act of atonement. Man could not perform a human act of infinite atonement, but Jesus Christ could. Whether he acted in his divine nature or in his human nature, it was the person, God, who acted. Hence he could offer infinite satisfaction or atonement for all human acts of rebellion.
*Reconciling the human race:* "When we were enemies we were reconciled to God by the death of his Son." (Romans 5:10.)

QUESTION 43: **Did this act of sacrifice restore to man what he had lost by sin: namely, supernatural life?**
ANSWER: The Church teaches that Jesus Christ by his suffering and death, merited for all men the supernatural life of grace, restoring man to divine sonship, and placing heaven once more within his reach.
*Merited for all:* That is, purchased for all men. "Christ died for all." (2 Cor. 5:15.)
*Supernatural life:* "I am come that men may have life, and have it more abundantly." (Jn. 10:10.)

*Heaven within reach: "You have received the spirit of adoption of sons . . . and if sons, heirs also; heirs indeed of God, and co-heirs with Christ." (Rom.8:15,17).*

QUESTION 44: **Did Jesus Christ provide the means whereby all men could receive the benefits of his redemption?**
ANSWER: Jesus Christ provided the means whereby all men should receive the benefits which he merited for them, by establishing his Church; to whom he gave his own divine authority to teach, rule, and sanctify all men unto the end of time.*Divine authority to teach all men: "Go ye therefore, teach all nations." (Mt. 28:19.) "He that heareth you, heareth me; and he that despiseth you, despiseth me." (Lk. 10:6.)*
*Divine authority to rule: "Teaching them to observe all things whatsoever I have commanded you." (Mt. 28:20.)*
*To sanctify: Through the divinely instituted sacraments of life, and participation in his sacrifice.*

QUESTION 45: **Is it only in and through this Church that man can obtain the supernatural life which is necessary for his destiny?**
ANSWER: Only in the Church and through the Church can men obtain the necessary supernatural life, since Jesus Christ neither indicated nor provided any other arrangement.

QUESTION 46: **What then is the complete definition of man as he is, as God sees him, as the Church must regard him, the subject of the particular rights and duties which we are about to discuss?**
ANSWER: Man is an individual person, possessing a human nature, made up of body (which is material) and soul (which is spiritual and immortal), created by God for a supernatural destiny, but born into the world deprived of the necessary supernatural life (through the sin of Adam), yet enabled to acquire the supernatural life (through the merits of Christ) under the conditions and in the manner laid down by God—that is, through the Church divinely instituted: (a) To teach God's truths to men; (b) to expound God's laws to men; (c) to convey God's life to men—whose life in this world is a probation, which will have an end, of which he must give an account, and for which eternal happiness or eternal punishment awaits him.
*Such then is man, a human being, called to supernatural happiness, and therefore to supernatural life, the subject of rights and duties, by nature and by grace.*

A CATHOLIC CATECHISM OF SOCIAL QUESTIONS

CHAPTER 6
LAW - MAN'S GUIDE TO HIS LAST END
AND THE MEASURE OF RIGHTS AND DUTIES

SECTION I: THE NATURAL LAW

QUESTION 47: What is the origin and source of law?
ANSWER: God created the whole universe for his own external glory. To attain this end God must have created the universe according to a general plan: the general plan is called God's eternal law.
*The universe: The complete subject of this law is the whole universe, embracing earth, heaven, hell. We are only concerned here with the visible universe.*
*General plan: This involves all parts of the visible universe—mineral, plant, animal, man—working together accomplishing one great end—the external glory of the Creator.*
*Eternal law: The plan of the eternal wisdom, accepted by the eternal will.*

QUESTION 48: **Since the things that make up the universe are varied and of different natures, how can they fulfill a common purpose?**
ANSWER: God gives to each a particular end to be attained, a perfection to be realized in accordance with its nature; by achieving this perfection each fulfills its own particular end, and promotes at the same time the perfection and end of the whole universe.

QUESTION 49: **How are the various elements of the universe connected with their particular ends?**
ANSWER: God, in creating them, created them with a tendency towards their own particular end—that is, he implanted in their nature or being a tendency by which they seek out and strive after their own end or perfection. The whole of these tendencies or strivings of created things is a sharing in what is called the eternal law.

QUESTION 50: **Do all created things share in the eternal law in the same way?**
ANSWER: No. Though all created things are subject to the eternal law as found in their nature, all created things have not the same nature. Some of those creatures have reason and free will. The manner in which the eternal law functions will not be identical for both irrational and rational creatures.

QUESTION 51: How does the eternal law function in irrational creatures?
ANSWER: The eternal law leads irrational creatures to their end by physical necessity.
*Irrational creatures: Brute beasts, plants, minerals, wind, rain, fire, water, stars, etc.*
*By physical necessity: They are directed and carried forward to the realization of their particular ends. They do what they must do. It is part of their nature that they are necessarily determined to their end, which they reach inevitably.*

QUESTION 52: How does the eternal law lead rational creatures to their end?
ANSWER: The eternal law leads men to their end by moral obligation: the reflection of this law in the reason of man is called the natural law.
*Moral obligation: Man is directed, but not carried forward to his end. He has intellect and free will; he must pursue the end of his nature according to his nature—that is, he must freely choose what will lead him to his end. He can choose to act in accord with the law of his being or go against it.*
*Natural Law: It is the law of nature properly so called, since only a creature with free will can really obey a law.*

QUESTION 53: How is man made aware of the natural law within himself which is to lead him to his end?
ANSWER: Man is made aware of the natural law of his being by the light of reason.
*By light of reason: As the animal by its natural instinct perceives what is good for it, so man by his reason estimates what is conducive to his end, and is thus directed. Whether he accepts that direction and moves towards that end depends on his free will.*
*Made aware of the natural law: Man's reason enables him to discover the law, but does not invent the law. Reason points out that the law is there (in man's nature) and what the law says; but it does not make the law, it only makes it known.*

QUESTION 54: Is it not generally accepted that it is the work of man's conscience to direct him to his end?
ANSWER: Yes. It is conscience which directs man, but conscience is not a faculty distinct from reason; it is reason, dictating practical judgments concerning the lawfulness or unlawfulness of definite particular acts.
*Practical judgments: (a) It informs man of the lawfulness or unlawfulness of*

*an act which he contemplates doing: (b) it dictates to his will the moral obligation of doing the act or of omitting it.*

QUESTION 55: **What is the first obligation of the natural law as far as man is concerned?**
ANSWER: The first obligation which the natural law imposes on man is the duty to do good and avoid evil, and to use his reason to learn what is good and what is evil.
*To use his reason to learn: Exercise his intellect, reflect, even study. His perception of the law may be clouded or dimmed by ignorance, prejudice, or passion. Since his reason is not infallible, it needs some instruction and education.*

QUESTION 56: **How can man set about discovering what is good or evil for him?**
ANSWER: By considering his relations with (a) his Creator, (b) himself, and (c) other creatures.
*Creator: Related to God as creature to Creator, depending on God for all that he is and all that he has.*
*Himself: Having faculties or powers of soul and body, demanding relationship to each other and the harmony of order.*
*Other creatures: Irrational creatures made for man and man's use and under man's dominion. To rational creatures he is related by social ties.*

QUESTION 57: **Who are the subjects of the natural law?**
ANSWER: The subjects of the natural law are all creatures possessing a rational nature—that is, all human beings.
*Rational nature: The law is universal in that it applies to all human beings. Individual men may sometimes be unable to use a particular faculty, but they do not cease to be men. They still have human nature, and it is in human nature that the natural law is founded. Human nature being common to all men, the natural law is universal, and therefore embraces infants, the feeble-minded, the physically defective, the incurable, the insane.*

QUESTION 58: **What is the nature of the precepts contained in the natural law?**
ANSWER: The natural law contains three kinds of precepts, which are known as primary, secondary, and tertiary precepts.
*Primary precepts: General truths, perceived immediately, of which no man with the use of reason can be ignorant, e.g., good must be done, evil avoided.*
*Secondary precepts: Which are easily deduced from the primary, e.g., children*

must honor parents. Men may be ignorant of these through carelessness, bad customs, or corrupt habits, but the ignorance is not without blame.
*Tertiary precepts:* Those less easily deduced from the first two classes, e.g., men must love their enemies. Of these it is possible for men to be ignorant without blame.

QUESTION 59: **Can any human power change the natural law?**
ANSWER: The natural law cannot be changed by any human power, whether of individuals or of society.
*Cannot be changed: Immutable.* No one but the lawmaker can alter the law. God created man, gave him his nature and purpose. God wills that man attain his end by the law of his nature implanted in his nature. To attempt to change the natural law is to attempt to change the will of God.
*Neither individuals nor society have power:* Though the state and the Church have authority from God to make laws, that authority only extends to the making of laws that recognize, harmonize with, and supplement the natural. Any society that attempts to alter the natural law acts beyond its powers, violates man's nature, and sets itself against the divine will.

QUESTION 60: **Can man ever escape from the natural law?**
ANSWER: Man can never escape from the natural law: that is, he can never escape from its binding force.
*Cannot escape from natural law:* It is founded in human nature, and is binding on every human being, whether that being approves of it or not. Man therefore cannot free himself from the natural law and its binding force. Man cannot change his human nature, nor set aside the law of his nature. He cannot suppress nor suspend the natural law. He cannot grant himself emancipation nor dispensation from the natural law. God is the author of man's nature and of the law of man's nature. Man himself is powerless to alter either or both.

QUESTION 61: **What happens if man chooses to ignore or defy the natural law, and acts against it?**
ANSWER: If man defies the natural law and acts against it, he does not destroy the law, but by breaking the law of his nature commits an offence against the Creator (sin), for which he is answerable to the Creator, and for which he will be punished.
*An illustration from physical laws:* Man is made up of body and soul. Man, having a body which is material, is subject to the ordinary physical laws which govern all material things. One of these physical laws is that bodies left unsupported will fall downwards to the earth and not upwards. Now if a

man chooses to ignore or defy this law and step off the roof of a house he is picked up damaged or a corpse. *The law is not destroyed, but man himself suffers damage or destruction.* Similarly, when man violates the moral or natural law he does not destroy the law, but he himself suffers damage or punishment, which punishment will only be adequate at the end of man's life.

SECTION 2: DIVINE POSITIVE LAW

QUESTION 62: **Is the natural law all that man needs to attain his end?**
ANSWER: No. Man needs positive law also, for many reasons.
*Many reasons:* Man's intellect may err in applying principles. It may be misled by custom, inclination, or surroundings. He needs further direction. Again, the well-being of men in general necessitates positive law to determine and govern rights and duties of individuals to promote the common good of all. Again, man's circumstances change, and his course amid new and changing circumstances is sometimes insufficiently indicated by the law of nature. Positive law will direct him amid all changing circumstances. This positive direction may come from God or from man. Thus man has, besides natural law, positive law, both divine and human, to enable him to reach his end.

QUESTION 63: **What is the principal reason for man's need of revealed positive law from God?**
ANSWER: The principal reason is this: Man's destiny is a supernatural destiny, concerning which the natural law is silent. Man needs therefore from God a revealed positive statement of the law by which his destiny is to be attained.
*Supernatural destiny:* We have seen already that man has not a natural destiny, but a supernatural one. Moreover, as man has only one life in which to attain that end, his whole life must be directed by the laws of supernatural life and purpose.
*Natural Law* is silent concerning supernatural life and destiny, because both are above human nature, not due to human nature. The natural law, therefore, is incomplete and insufficient for man's end. He needs a statement from God of the laws of supernatural life and purpose.

QUESTION 64: **Has God always provided the human race with the divine positive law which is necessary if men are to attain their supernatural destiny?**

ANSWER: From the beginning man has had the divine positive law of life and destiny before him.

*From the beginning:* (a) When God made our first parents he revealed to them the law by which they would reach their supernatural destiny. He promulgated positive laws regarding man's conduct to his Creator, his neighbor, and himself, as is clearly indicated in Genesis, Chapter 1. (b) To Moses God gave the commandments, which were a more abundant and emphatic promulgation of man's duties as already contained in the natural law, that many had lost sight of.

QUESTION 65: When God the Son became man did he give any new law to men?

ANSWER: Jesus Christ promulgated a new law by which men were to make the journey of life and reach their supernatural destiny.

*A new law:* (a) Christ took the Ten Commandments and summed them up into two— "Thou shalt love the Lord thy God with thy whole heart," and "Thou shalt love thy neighbor as thyself." On these two commandments, the whole law is based. Love, then, is the source of all law. Law is love. (b) He taught that mere external observance of the law (as shown in the Pharisees) was not enough, and he emphasized internal obedience to the law. The root of action is mind or heart, and sins of thought or desire are as serious as sinful actions. (c) Christ revealed a whole body of detailed laws or rules whereby the love of God and of our neighbor are to be shown. This body of rules or laws Christ entrusted to his Church, from whom alone can men learn what is contained therein.

QUESTION 66: If men wish to attain their supernatural destiny must they accept the law of Christ as taught by his Church?

ANSWER: Yes, that is God's arrangement, which all men are obliged to accept.

*God's arrangement:* Christ established his Church for one purpose only, namely to teach men infallibly the truths of life's meaning and purpose and guide them unerringly to their final destiny.

*Men obliged to accept:* Because the Church is the sole, authorized, and divinely appointed guide for all men, for all time, in the way of salvation.

QUESTION 67: What is the scope of the Church's power with regard to God's laws?

ANSWER: The Church is the interpreter of the natural law; she is the interpreter and promulgator of the divine positive law; and she is empowered to make laws of her own.

*Natural law:* To the Church belongs the right to say what is contained in the natural law.

*Divine positive law:* Of this the Church is the divinely appointed custodian, interpreter, and promulgator.

*Laws of her own:* The Church cannot alter God's law, whether it be the natural law or divine positive law, yet within the framework of God's law she can make by-laws, and with God's authority; e.g., she requires the presence of a priest for Catholic marriage. These bylaws, being her own, she can alter, but she cannot alter God's law, nor has she any desire to do so.

QUESTION 68: **Does the new law which Christ gave to his Church contain all the guidance that man needs for the supernatural life?**
ANSWER: The new law which God gave to the Church covers all the duties that arise from man's relations with God, himself, and other men in the supernatural order.

*Relations in supernatural order:* (a) To God the Father as a son; (b) To God the Son as a member of his body, i.e., the Church; (c) to God the Holy Ghost as the temple in which he dwells.

*Within himself:* His faculties must be subjected by grace to God.

*With other men:* Related as co-heirs of the same kingdom in the brotherhood of sons of a common Father who is in heaven.

QUESTION 69: **What are men obliged to do by the new law which God promulgates through the Church?**
ANSWER: The new law promulgated by the Church with God's authority imposes on all such an obligation to work to obtain their supernatural destiny.

*All men:* The divine positive law is binding on all men for all time, and all must submit to it.

*To work:* "With fear and trembling work out your salvation." (Phil. 2:12.)

QUESTION 70: **What is comprised in this fundamental obligation on man to work towards the realization of his last end?**
ANSWER: Man must (a) acknowledge God in theory and in practice as his ultimate end; (b) he must work positively—that is, do good.

*Acknowledge God in theory and practice:* Therefore must reject everything that makes that end impossible—that is, he must avoid sin. He must believe in God, hope in him, and love him.

*Work positively:* Firstly, he must receive Baptism. "Unless a man be born *again of water and the Holy Ghost he cannot enter the kingdom of heaven."* (Jn. 3:5.) Secondly, he must observe the commandments. *"If thou wilt enter into life keep the commandments."* (Mt. 19:17.) Thirdly, should he lose his claim to his last end by sin, he is bound to regain it by Penance.

QUESTION 71: **Does the Church then displace man's conscience?**
ANSWER: Man's conscience is not displaced by the Church; the Church by her teaching renders his conscience properly instructed, and gives man a clear perception of the law and its obligation, enabling man to follow his conscience unswervingly.

*Conscience properly instructed: Man's conscience is his reason, which is capable of, and needs, instruction. The Church gives man God's own instructions on law and life. Man has therefore the highest enlightenment possible in this life.*

QUESTION 72: **Has God given any sanction to his laws?**
ANSWER: God has given a sanction with his laws which makes them holy; this sanction is the reward of Heaven for all who observe them, and the punishment of hell for those who break them.

*Reward and punishment: God has made this sanction so clear to men that any doubt on the matter is impossible.*

QUESTION 73: **Are all men called to perfection, and have they an ideal of perfection to which they should aspire?**
ANSWER: Man, by the natural law, is obliged to attain perfection. It is also commanded by Jesus Christ ("Be ye therefore perfect"—Mt. 5:48), and Jesus Christ himself is the ideal.

*Man's perfection and ideal: The only type of goodness in the present order is Christian goodness. The only ideal of perfection in the present order is the Christian ideal—Jesus Christ. He came to show men the way to heaven by example as well as teaching. The domestic society of the family and the civil society of their fellowmen will assist men to attain perfection and their last end, but Jesus Christ alone is the Leader and Master in the way of perfection. He commands men: "Follow me, I am the way, the truth, and the life." He gave men not only divine commands, but also divine counsels. By co-operation with the divine aid all men of goodwill can attain moral perfection, as shown in their model—Jesus Christ. To this perfection men are obliged to rise and acquire the essential resemblance to Christ, who, being God, for man's sake became man.*

LIFE

# Part II

## The Teaching of the Church on Particular Rights and Duties

CHAPTER 7
LIFE

SECTION I: REGARDING ONE´S OWN LIFE

QUESTION 74: **To whom belongs the complete and absolute dominion over man's life?**
ANSWER: Since the principle of life in man is his soul (Q. 17), and since every human soul is created by God (Q. 18), all human life is under the complete and absolute dominion of God.
*Dominion: The power or authority to rule, govern, or control persons or things.*
*Absolute dominion: God alone is the absolute master of life and death.*

QUESTION 75: **Has not man dominion over his own life?**
ANSWER: Every man has dominion over his own life, but it is only a limited and qualified dominion.
*Qualified dominion: Man has the administration or stewardship of his life, but he is only free to administer reasonably. He may only use his life in accordance with his rational nature and the law of his nature. (Q. 52.)*

QUESTION 76: **What is the first duty with regard to one's own life?**
ANSWER: Every human being receives his life from the Creator, and the natural law imposes on each the duty of preserving and developing that life according to the purpose of the Creator.

QUESTION 77: **How much is embraced by this fundamental duty?**
ANSWER: This fundamental duty embraces the obligation to preserve his own life, health, and bodily integrity, and to secure those things which are necessary for that purpose, namely food, clothing, and shelter.
*Bodily integrity: Man must keep his body whole and entire as God made it.*

QUESTION 78: **How far is a man bound to preserve life?**
ANSWER: Man is bound to take the ordinary means to preserve life and health.

*Ordinary means: To be judged by the common estimation of men. Man is not bound to take extraordinary means, e.g., to undergo an operation fraught with grave danger.*

*Men are bound to avoid proximate dangers to life; but not remote dangers, because to do the latter would make life impossible.*

*It is lawful to expose oneself to proximate danger to life when duty requires it, or some higher good demands it, e.g., a priest may have to risk his life for the spiritual good of others.*

*Mortification, fasting, penance, etc., are lawful and praiseworthy, since they are undergone for a higher good.*

QUESTION 79: **Is suicide clearly an unlawful act?**
ANSWER: Suicide, that is the direct and spontaneous compassing of one's own death, is a crime against the natural law and divine positive law.

*Against natural law: Because the creature thereby usurps God's authority over life. To claim power to destroy a thing is to claim full dominion over that thing. Only God has full dominion over life.*

*Against divine positive law: "Thou shalt not kill." (Ex. 20:13; Deut. 5:17; Mt. 5:21.)*

*The Church refuses Christian burial to such a one.*

QUESTION 80: **Is there not a growing opinion that a man may be justified, in exceptional circumstances, in taking his life, as for example when he becomes a victim of great suffering, or incurably diseased, or becomes a burden to others, or useless to others?**
ANSWER: None of these motives, nor any other motive, can ever justify such a grave violation of the natural and divine law as the deliberate taking of one's own life and the usurping of the Creator's right and authority over life and death.

*No motive can justify: Such motives are based on false sentiment and a false idea of life and its value. The value of a human life is not to be reckoned by its usefulness to others. Every life, in every condition, and at all times, retains its chief purpose, namely the meriting of eternal life, for which God created it.*

QUESTION 81: Does the moral law forbid mutilation or injury to oneself without just reason?
ANSWER: The mutilation of oneself without just reason is a violation of the natural law and divine positive law.

*Against natural law: The natural law demands that man must use his members for the benefit of the whole body, its life, perfection, and well-being.*

*Against divine positive law: The command "Thou shalt not kill" forbids mutilation of oneself.*

*Against natural and divine positive law: Christian doctrine establishes, and the light of reason makes it most clear, that individuals have no power over the members of their bodies than that which pertains to their natural ends; and they are not free to destroy or mutilate their members or in any way, render themselves unfit for their natural functions, except when no other provision can be made for the good of the whole body" (Pius XI, Encyclical Letter Casti Connubii, December 31, 1930).*

QUESTION 82: What would be a just reason for consenting to the mutilation of one's own body or members?
ANSWER: It is only lawful to allow mutilation of oneself when such action is necessary to preserve health and life.

*Necessary to preserve life: Among physical goods the greatest is life itself. There is no offence against law in allowing the mutilation of the body or sacrificing a member of the body in order to save what is better than any part of it, namely life itself. Thus it is no violation of the natural law to cut away diseased flesh or a diseased member.*

QUESTION 83: Is it lawful to allow or to undergo an operation or mutilation which results in a state of sterility?
ANSWER: It is lawful to allow or undergo such an operation when it is the only and necessary means of preserving the health of the individual, milder measures being insufficient.

QUESTION 84: Is it lawful to allow sterilization, that is, is it lawful to undergo an operation for the express purpose of inducing sterility which will render future propagation impossible?
ANSWER: To undergo such an operation expressly for the purpose of inducing sterility, thus making propagation impossible, is forbidden by natural and divine positive law.

A CATHOLIC CATECHISM OF SOCIAL QUESTIONS

SECTION 2: REGARDING THE LIFE OF OTHERS

QUESTION 85: **Must all men respect the right to live which each individual possesses?**
ANSWER: Since every human being receives life from God (Q. 18), every human being has a God-given right to live, and this right involves a corresponding duty on all others to respect that right.

QUESTION 86: **Is it unlawful to take away the life of another human being?**
ANSWER: The moral law forbids the killing of any human being without the intervention of a legitimate authority.
*Any human being: The unborn child, the weakly infant, the unwanted child, the defective physically or mentally, the insane, etc., are all subjects of the natural law (Q. 57), and each one possesses the right to live (Q. 85).*
*Consequently, direct killing of unborn child, directly induced abortion, are crimes against natural and divine positive law.*
*Those also share the guilt who participate in these crimes by their counsel, aid, assistance, or any other means.*
*Without legitimate authority: That is, by a private person. It may be (a) murder, i.e., deliberate killing, or (b) culpable homicide, due to negligence or carelessness, and to which blame is attached.*

QUESTION 87: **What is to be said of euthanasia, as advocated by moderns?**
ANSWER: The direct application of euthanasia, that is the direct compassing of painless death (by administering an overdose of morphine or any other product of the "lethal chamber") is forbidden by natural and divine positive law.
*Euthanasia forbidden: Every human being has a right to life, which right is inalienable, that is, cannot be surrendered. The direct taking of the life of another is a crime against the moral law (Q. 86), no matter how humane and painless the method of killing may be.*

QUESTION 88: **Is it lawful to injure or even kill another in self-defense?**
ANSWER: Since man is bound to safeguard and protect life, it is lawful to take such means in defense of one's own life as may result in the death or mutilation of an unjust aggressor, but the means taken must be in proportion to the danger.

*Unjust aggressor: An aggressor is unjust when he has no proper authority to punish.*
*Lawful to take means: That one's defense be without blame three conditions are required—(a) danger must be imminent, i.e., simultaneous with attack; (b) act of defense may not exceed force of attack; only damage sufficient to ward off danger is permissible. Therefore a person is bound to take the other possible means, e.g., warn assailant, call for help, or escape if possible; (c) the intention must simply be self-defense, the result to the aggressor—either death or injury—is a second effect, permitted, but not intended.*
*Proportionate to danger: Some goods or possessions are comparable to life itself, e.g., integrity of limbs, chastity, a considerable fortune, etc.*

QUESTION 89: **Has the state the right to inflict punishment, particularly capital punishment?**
ANSWER: In the interests of the common good the state has the right and the necessary authority from God to punish and even deprive a person of life as a just punishment for crime committed.
*State has the right by natural law: Since the state has all the means necessary and God's authority to preserve the common good of all; and by divine positive law—"The ruler is God's minister for good in thy regard, but if thou dost evil, be afraid, for he beareth not the sword in vain" (Rom.13:4).*
*Authority from God: "Let every soul be subject to higher powers. For there is no power but from God, and those that are exist by God's arrangement" (Rom. 13:1).*

QUESTION 90: **Is lynching against the moral law?**
ANSWER: The authority to punish or execute a person guilty of crime belongs to the state, and only those who have been properly commissioned may carry out the sentence—hence lynching is forbidden by the moral law.
*Properly commissioned: Even if a criminal has forfeited his right to life, and is already under judicial sentence of death, no private person or persons may assume authority to carry out the sentence. Lynching is murder. (Q. 86.).*

QUESTION 91: **What is to be said of legalized or state sterilization of defectives?**
ANSWER: Legalized sterilization, for the sole purpose of preventing defectives from procreating, is against the law and divine positive law.
*Against natural law: Integrity of body is an inalienable right. The state oversteps its authority in inflicting grave mutilation.*
*Against divine positive law: "Public magistrates have no right over the*

*bodies of their subjects; therefore where no crime has taken place, and there is no cause present for grave punishment, they can never directly harm or tamper with the integrity of the body, either for reasons of eugenics or for another reason." (Letter of Pius XI, Encyclical Casti Connubii, December 31, 1930.)*

*The state has authority to punish, but only when crime has been committed (Q. 89). To be defective is not a crime. To have the power of propagating is not a crime. Therefore the state may not interfere with life or limb of such a person, nor punish (by sterilization) when no crime has been committed*

QUESTION 92: **Is it unlawful to expose others to danger to life and health?**
ANSWER: Since all men have a duty to preserve life, health, and bodily integrity (Q. 77), employers are bound by natural law to respect life, health, and integrity of limbs which their employees possess.

*By natural law: It is immoral to expose workers to grave danger without proper safeguards. It is immoral to tax workers beyond their strength, or employ them in work unsuited to their age or sex.*

QUESTION 93: **Is it only the actual committing of these offences that is forbidden by the moral law?**
ANSWER: The moral law forbids not only the actual committing of all these offences, but forbids likewise all intention and even desire to commit them; moreover, the indulging in unruly passions, e.g., hatred, anger, revenge, etc., from which serious offences arise, is forbidden by the moral law.

*Hatred, anger, revenge: "Whoever hateth his brother is a murderer." (1 Jn. 3:15) Since hatred is forbidden by the moral law, it follows that a commandment is given of charity and love. Class war is clearly immoral. "Have peace with all men." (Rom. 12:18.) Class hatred and class warfare stand condemned by the whole life of our Lord Jesus Christ and by his teaching.*

CHAPTER 8

EDUCATION

QUESTION 94: **To whom belongs the responsibility for the rearing of children?**
ANSWER: By natural law and divine positive law the responsibility for the rearing of a child belongs to the parents of the child.

*Parents responsibility: This office, which embraces a duty and a right to rear the child, comes to the parents directly from God. The rearing of a child is the building up and training of the child in body and mind.*

QUESTION 95: **What is meant by the education of a child?**
ANSWER: The education of a child is that part of the rearing of a child which relates to the information of mind, and the formation of character.
*Information of mind: That is, the instruction of the intellect, and imparting of knowledge necessary and useful.*
*Formation of character: That is, the training of the will in the choice and pursuit of moral goodness.*
*To love the "good" is as essential as to know the "truth". Any system of education which ignores this twofold character of education is unsound and defective.*

QUESTION 96: **On whom rests the responsibility for the education of the child?**
ANSWER: On the parents falls directly the responsibility of educating the child of the marriage.
*Parents directly responsible: This duty and right which comes to them directly from God, is not, however, absolute and despotic, but qualified, that is, parents are not free to do absolutely as they like with the education of their children, but must exercise their right in conformity with the purpose for which God gave life (Q. 22 & 23), and in accord with natural and divine law. There is a further duty imposed on parents of preventing any invasion of their rights in this matter.*

QUESTION 97: **What is the aim and purpose of true education?**
ANSWER: Recalling the definition of man (Q. 46), it is clear that the aim and purpose of true education is to transform the child into the supernatural man who will think, judge, and act consistently in accord with right reason illumined by supernatural light; and in accord with the example and teaching of Jesus Christ which is given us by the Church.
*Supernatural light: Man must be endowed with supernatural or sanctifying grace with its accompanying virtues, particularly faith, which illumines the mind.*
*Example and teaching of Christ: Christ came to redeem and save us (Q. 43), and to teach us the way to heaven.*
*Given by the Church: The Church is our immediate or proximate rule of faith*

*(Q. 4). Faith here embraces faith and morals, i.e., what we must believe and what we must do.*

QUESTION 98: **What is the essential character of true education?**
ANSWER: In view of the definition of man (Q. 46), and in view of the aim and purpose of true education (Q. 97), it is clear that education must have an essentially religious character.

*Education essentially religious: Education is above all else the training and development of character. The will can only be trained by reference to a fixed standard of moral conduct; and there can be no sound and consistent morality without religion and living religious principles.*

*Education without religion means education with the chief subject left out. Education which is divorced from religion is against the natural law.*

QUESTION 99: **Is environment a necessary and important factor in Christian education?**
ANSWER: The proper environment is a necessary and important factor in Christian education.

*Proper environment: Religion must form the background, and as it were the atmosphere in which youth is educated. The conditions which surround the child must be in keeping with the purpose and end of education.*

QUESTION 100: **Where should this proper environment be found in the first instance?**
ANSWER: The first and necessary element of this environment must be found in the family and the home.

*Family and home: The value of a well ordered and disciplined Christian family cannot be overestimated as regards its good influence on the child. The good example of parents and other members of the family supply the best training and effective education of the child.*

QUESTION 101: **Does not the Church supply a divinely instituted environment for the Christian education of youth?**
ANSWER: The Church is divinely established to teach all men and direct them to their last end (Q. 44), therefore she is the educational environment most intimately connected with the child and the family.

*Environment of the Church: The Church is the custodian and teacher of the whole of moral truth (Q. 68), and dispenser of the sacraments which give life and grace; elevating and educating her children by means of her sacred liturgy and ritual, and by religious associations that increase and foster piety.*

QUESTION 102: Is the school a necessary institution and an important factor in the education of youth?

ANSWER: Since children must be equipped to take their place in life and in civil society, and since the family is generally unable of itself to supply the necessary instruction in arts and sciences, the school becomes a necessary institution, and constitutes an added and important environment in the education of youth.

*School is necessary: In its origin the school came into existence through the family and the Church, and was intended to be complementary to the family and the Church. The school, therefore, in its policy and environment, should form one sanctuary of education with the family and the Church.*

QUESTION 103: What right does the state possess in the matter of the education of youth?

ANSWER: Since the state exists to promote the common temporal welfare, the state has the right (and the authority) to see that children are educated by those responsible, and, moreover, to see that they are educated in such a way as to make them good and useful citizens.

QUESTION 104: Has the state an absolute right over the education of children?

ANSWER: The state has no absolute right, but only a relative and qualified right over the education of children.

*No absolute right: The child does not belong to the state. The child only becomes a member of the state through the family. Both the child and the parents have rights in the matter of education which cannot be surrendered, which the state must respect, and may not set aside. Hence the state cannot have an absolute right over the education of children.*

*Relative and qualified right: The state, no less than individuals, must observe the natural and divine law which give to the parents priority of right over the education of the children. Hence, whatever right the state possesses in the matter of education is relative to or qualified by the already established rights of parents and child.*

QUESTION 105: What precisely is the duty of the state regarding the education of youth?

ANSWER: It is the duty of the state (1) to see that the parents fulfill their duty of educating their children, and (2) to supplement and support their efforts and to supply their deficiencies.

*To see that parents fulfill their duty:* Should parents fail through neglect or incapacity or be found wanting either physically or morally in respect to the education of their children, then it is the duty of the state to protect the rights of the children and provide for their education.

*To supplement and support their efforts:* Should the efforts of the parents fall short of what is necessary, the state must supplement their work out of her own resources, e.g., by providing facilities, or even buildings if necessary. The whole community places these means and resources at the disposal of the state for the needs of the whole community. The state should distribute them justly and without prejudice, respecting at the same time the rights of the family and of the Church.

QUESTION 106: How far do the respective rights of Church and state extend over the education of the child?

ANSWER: The rights of Church and state in the field of education are defined by the purpose for which the Church and the state exist, and for which both derive authority from God.

*Defined by the purpose of Church and state:* The purpose of the Church is the eternal welfare of men. The authority and therefore the rights of the Church extend to whatever is sacred in human life and whatever pertains to the worship of God and the attaining of man's eternal destiny. Hence the Church has the right to decide what kind of education is necessary for man's eternal destiny.

*The purpose of the state is the temporal welfare of men.* The authority and rights of the state extend to what pertains to the common temporal well-being of the community. Hence there are limits to the authority of the state, and its rights in the field of education cannot trespass beyond its own sphere and purpose.

*Thus it is not the function of the state to teach religion:* this belongs to the Church. But the state has no right to prevent religion being taught, or to penalize (by refusing aid) those who desire it for their children.

QUESTION 107: Is it a grave injustice to prevent or hamper the teaching of religion in school?

ANSWER: It is a grave violation of natural and divine law to hamper or hinder or reject the teaching of religion in school. Those who attempt such a policy violate the rights of God, the rights of the Church, the rights of the parents, and the rights of the child.

*The rights of God:* Every creature is created by God for eternal life. He who hinders the attaining of that eternal life violates the rights of God.

*The rights of the Church:* The Church has a divine mission to ensure the *eternal salvation of men. This cannot be achieved without religious education in school.*

*The rights of parents: The state and the school are only deputies of the parents in the matter of education. Hence they deputize for the parents, but do not displace them. No power can justly take from parents their right to educate their children according to their conscience.*

*The rights of the child: The child has a right to know its destiny, and to be helped in every way to attain it.*

QUESTION 108: What is the teaching of the Church regarding "naturalism" in education?

ANSWER: The Church condemns every system of education which has its foundation and inspiration in naturalism.

*Naturalism: By naturalism is understood any outlook on life and life's purpose which excludes or ignores supernatural truth, supernatural law, or supernatural life. Naturalism is false and unsound because (a) it rejects the true definition of man's nature and purpose (Q. 46), (b) it rejects the doctrine of Original Sin and its effects in all men (Questions 34–37), (c) it rejects or ignores the doctrine of grace (Q. 43), (d) it sets aside the authority of God and his divine law (Questions 69, 70), (e) it ignores the natural law which reason itself promulgates (Q. 53). The general principle of naturalism is that man can only rely on, and be guided solely by the unaided powers of human nature. Its disciples preach "self-expression", and aim at "emancipating" men from law, which they describe as "obsolete" and "old-fashioned". The logical result of such teaching is that men are made slaves of their own pride and passions, which in due course must lead to chaos and to the destruction of the individual and of society.*

QUESTION 109: What does the Church teach regarding the system of education known as "co-education"?

ANSWER: The principle of co-education is condemned by the Church as having its foundation, among its advocates, on naturalism and the denial of Original sin.

*Co-education: By this is to be understood the policy or system which would treat boys and girls as if they were the same, and which advocates the indiscriminate mixing of them not only in classes, but in recreation, physical training, and all other activities.*

*Condemned by the Church: because, based on naturalism and the denial of Original Sin and its consequences (Q. 108). Furthermore, by nature the two sexes are different in organism, in temperament, and in aptitude; hence there should not be any leveling promiscuity nor equality in the training of the different sexes. There should be distinction and separation of scholars particularly during those years which form the most delicate and decisive period in the formation of character.*

QUESTION 110: **Does the mere fact that a school gives some religious instruction satisfy the claims of Christian education?**
ANSWER: The mere fact that a school gives some religious instruction does not satisfy the rights of the family and of the Church, nor make it a suitable place for Catholic children.
*Does not satisfy:* "It is necessary not only that religious instruction be given to the young at certain fixed times, but also that every other subject taught be permeated with Christian piety. If this is wanting, if this sacred atmosphere does not pervade and warm the hearts of masters and scholars alike, little good can be expected from any kind of learning, and considerable harm will often be the consequence." *(Leo XIII, Encyclical letter, Militantis Ecclesiae, August 1, 1897.)*

QUESTION 111: **Are Catholic parents forbidden to send their children to non-Catholic schools?**
ANSWER: The law of the Church expressly forbids Catholic parents to send their children to non-Catholic schools, whether those schools are "neutral" or "mixed".
*Neutral schools:* That is; schools from which religion is excluded. In practice there is no such thing as a school which merely holds itself aloof from religion, for, where religion is not taught, irreligion spreads and holds sway. "The school, if not a temple, is a den."
*Mixed schools:* That is, schools which are open to Catholics and non-Catholics alike, e.g., public schools in this country.
*Law of the Church expressly forbids:* Code of Canon Law, canon 1374. The law also declares that the bishop alone has the power to dispense from this law in determined circumstances and with necessary precautions.

QUESTION 112: **What is the ideal system of education for Catholics?**
ANSWER: There can be only one ideal of Catholic education, an ideal which must be aimed at and safeguarded even at the cost of great sacrifice. That ideal is Catholic education, in Catholic schools, by Catholic teachers, for all the Catholic youth.

QUESTION 113: **What position does the teacher hold in the Christian education of youth?**

ANSWER: The Christian teacher undertakes a grave responsibility, performing a service to God, to the child, to the family, to the Church, and to the state, and therefore should be held in honor and respect by the whole community.

*Grave responsibility:* The Christian teacher must recognize his or her work as a vocation and not merely as an occupation. Since good example is most important, much is expected of the Christian teacher, not only in school, but also outside school.

*Honor and respect:* Should be shown by everyone; by the state in remuneration, which will adequately express honor and respect for the greatest of public services; by parents, who, in the first place, must themselves show respect for the teacher, and in the second place, must insist on their children doing likewise.

QUESTION 114: **Does Catholic education make for good citizenship?**
ANSWER: The aim of Catholic education is to form good Catholics, and in doing so must necessarily form at the same time good citizens.

*The good Catholic necessarily a good citizen:* Catholic education devotes great attention and importance to the formation of character, respect for law and order, and obedience to legitimate authority. Consequently, Catholic education furnishes the best possible preparation for good citizenship.

CHAPTER 9

MARRIAGE

QUESTION 115: **How did the institution of marriage arise?**
ANSWER: Marriage was instituted and established by God himself when he made our first parents.

*Instituted by God himself:* Therefore it is not the invention or work of man, but was divinely instituted by the Creator, who also established its essential properties and fixed its purpose.

*Our first parents:* God established Adam and Eve as husband and wife, and decreed that the human race should be propagated through divinely instituted wedlock. (Gen. 2.)

QUESTION 116: **What was the nature of marriage as instituted by God in the beginning?**
ANSWER: Marriage, as instituted by God in the beginning, was a sacred permanent union of one man and one woman as husband and wife.

*A sacred union:* Sacred, because the marriage bond is forged by God, receives its sanction from God, and is blessed by God.
*A permanent union:* See Q. 119.
*One man and one woman:* "Moses by reason of the hardness of your heart permitted you to put away your wives, but from the beginning it was not so." (Mt. 19:8.) Therefore marriage as instituted by God in the beginning was a union of one man and one woman, to the exclusion of any third party.
*As husband and wife:* With a new and most intimate relationship, from which arise mutual rights and duties.

QUESTION 117: **For what purpose was marriage instituted by God?**
ANSWER: The end of human beings is the glory of God and their eternal happiness with God (Q. 22 & 23); the final or ultimate purpose of marriage is to beget children for the glory of God and to enable them to share the happiness of heaven.
*Final or ultimate purpose:* Besides this ultimate end or purpose, marriage has its immediate ends, which are called primary and secondary.

QUESTION 118: **What are the immediate primary and secondary ends of marriage?**
ANSWER: By natural law and divine positive law the primary end or purpose of marriage is the procreation and education of children; and its secondary ends the mutual help, love, fidelity of husband and wife, and to be a safeguard against lust.
*By natural law:* Nature's purposes (both primary and secondary) in marriage are dictated by the nature of the two sexes, which are different in physical organism, in temperament, and in aptitude, and are meant to complement each other. The culmination of the relationship is reached in the birth of offspring.
*By divine positive law:* God proclaimed the primary purpose of marriage to be the propagation of the human race (Gen. xxvii, 28), and also its secondary purposes (Gen. ii, 18).

QUESTION 119: **Is marriage a permanent and indissoluble union?**
ANSWER: By natural law and divine positive law marriage is essentially permanent and indissoluble.
*Essentially:* i.e., a necessary quality or property of every marriage.
*Permanent:* i.e., not a temporary arrangement but a stable and lasting union. This is clear from the primary and secondary purposes of marriage (Q. 118). The education of a child takes many years, and nature intends not one

child but several. The secondary ends of marriage imperatively demand that the union be permanent and lifelong.

*Indissoluble: i.e., unbreakable.* The marriage bond cannot be loosed or severed either by the parties themselves or by any human power. Marriage is indissoluble by natural law because of its primary and secondary ends. When two persons contract to take each other in marriage it is God who joins them together. God alone can sever that bond, which he does in the death of one of the parties. By divine positive law marriage is indissoluble from its first institution. *(Mt. 19:4, 8.)*

QUESTION 120: **Was marriage preserved among men as God instituted it?**

ANSWER: Men (even the chosen race) lost to a certain extent the ideal of marriage as instituted by God, and presumed or were granted "because of the hardness of their hearts" plurality of wives, and even divorce.

QUESTION 121: **Did Jesus Christ condemn these abuses of marriage?**

ANSWER: Jesus Christ condemned the abuses of plurality of wives and divorce which had been tolerated, reasserting the unity and indissolubility of marriage; furthermore, he forbade any human power to interfere with marriage as instituted by God.

*Condemned abuses: Mt. 19:4, 8.*
*Reasserted unity: "Now they are not two, but one flesh."*
*Reasserted indissolubility: "What God hath joined together, let no man put asunder."*
*Forbade any human interference: whether of individuals or of the state.*

QUESTION 122: **What was the most important thing that Jesus Christ did for marriage?**

ANSWER: Jesus Christ raised the marriage of Christians to the dignity of a sacrament.

*Christian marriage a sacrament: That is, Jesus Christ made Christian marriage one of the channels by which the merits of his Passion and Death are conveyed to husband and wife. The marriage contract of Christians (i.e., those who have been baptized) is an outward sign, ordained by Jesus Christ, which not only signifies, but actually and effectively causes grace in their souls. In Christian marriage the contract is inseparable from the sacrament. If there is no true marriage contract (because some essential is wanting), there is no sacrament. If there is no sacrament there is no true marriage contract.*

QUESTION 123: **What are the effects of Christian marriage?**
ANSWER: In Christian marriage the contract and the sacrament are one and the same thing; the effects of the contract in it are (a) matrimonial rights and duties to each other; (b) rights and duties regarding the rearing and education of children; (c) married status and all the civil effects of such. The effects of the sacrament in it are (a) an increase of sanctifying grace, and (b) a title to actual graces from God.
*Increase of sanctifying grace: With its accompanying virtues, and therefore an increase of supernatural life. (Q. 28.)*
*Title to actual graces from God: i.e., they have a right or claim to supernatural power or help from God to fulfill their rights and duties faithfully, holily, perseveringly unto death.*

QUESTION 124: **To whom belongs the right to regulate and control Christian marriage?**
ANSWER: The right to regulate and control Christian marriage was given by Jesus Christ to his Church, and to her alone; therefore the Church has the exclusive right to regulate and control the marriage of Christians.
*Church has exclusive right: The Church is the sole custodian and legislator of the sacraments. Christian marriage is a sacrament; therefore the Church is the sole custodian and legislator of Christian marriage. Furthermore, the Church cannot share her authority in this matter with anyone else. The Church is infallible (Q. 9), and cannot err in claiming, as she has done since her foundation, the right to determine the conditions under which a Christian marriage must be contracted.*

QUESTION 125: **What precisely is the authority which the Church received from Jesus Christ with regard to marriage?**
ANSWER: The Church is authorized by Jesus Christ (a) to teach what is contained in the natural law regarding marriage, its nature, its properties, and its end; (b) to promulgate the divine positive law regarding marriage; (c) to make laws (within the framework of divine positive law) for the administration and reception of Christian marriage.

QUESTION 126: **Does the right and authority of the Church extend over all Christian marriages?**
ANSWER: The right and authority of the Church extends over all Christian marriages, that is over marriages of baptized persons, whether they actually submit to her authority or not.

*Right and authority over all Christian marriages: Because every Christian marriage is a sacrament: The Church sometimes exempts baptized non-Catholics from particular marriage laws, e.g., the law requiring the presence of a priest (Q. 128).*

QUESTION 127: Does the Church impose certain impediments to marriage? And why does she do so?
ANSWER: The Church in her marriage legislation imposes certain impediments which arise from natural law or divine positive law or from her own ecclesiastical law; some of these impediments or obstacles render a contemplated marriage impossible, others, though not making it impossible, render it unlawful.
*Unlawful: Unless a dispensation from the law is obtained. The Church can only dispense from impediments that arise from her own ecclesiastical laws. She cannot dispense from impediments that are dictated by the natural and divine positive laws.*
*Why impediments?: In order to protect each party to the marriage and to safeguard the contract and the sacrament.*

QUESTION 128: Must Catholics observe the laws of the Church in contracting marriage?
ANSWER: Catholics are bound to observe the laws of the Church in contracting marriage, which rule that the marriage of Catholics must take place in the presence of the bishop or the parish priest or a priest delegated by either and at least two witnesses—otherwise it is no marriage at all.
*Marriage of Catholics: (a) This law binds all Catholics; (b) it binds a Catholic who wishes to marry a non-Catholic; (c) it does not apply to marriages between non-Catholics.*

QUESTION 129: Does the Church allow and approve of "mixed marriages"?
ANSWER: The Church sometimes allows a Catholic to marry a baptized non-Catholic (that is, she grants a dispensation from her law forbidding a Catholic to marry a heretic or schismatic), but only for grave reasons, and under stipulated conditions. She never approves of them.
*Church allows: She tolerates such a union when she cannot prevent it.*
*For grave reasons: Usually in order to prevent a greater evil.*
*Under stipulated conditions: (a) The non-Catholic party must give a signed promise not to interfere with the religious belief or practice of the Catholic; (b)*

*both must give a signed promise to rear all children of the marriage in the Catholic religion.*

*The Church never approves: Because such a union (a) is opposed to the spiritual good of the Catholic partner and the children; (b) constituting a danger of perversion to Catholic partner and children; (c) and frequently resulting in great unhappiness, both earthly and eternal. The Church shows her disapproval by refusing to bless such unions.*

*What is said here applies with equal or even greater force when a Catholic chooses to marry an unbaptized person.*

QUESTION 130: **What does the Church teach regarding "civil marriages"?**
ANSWER: The Church teaches that between Christians marriage is always a sacrament and a religious act, so that between Christians there cannot be such a thing as a purely civil or non-sacramental marriage.

*Civil marriage: i.e., marriage contracted before a secular magistrate, or registrar, or justice of the peace.*

*Between Christians: (a) As between Catholics, the Church teaches that a civil marriage is no marriage at all; (b) as between baptized non-Catholics, the matrimonial contract, wheresoever made (in church, registry, hall, or house) constitutes them man and wife and confers on them the sacrament of Matrimony; (c) as regards the unbaptized, their marriage contract, wherever made, establishes them husband and wife; their marriage remains a natural or non-sacramental marriage.*

QUESTION 131: **Has the state any authority over the marriages of its subjects?**
ANSWER: The state has no authority over Christian marriage, but has authority to regulate the purely civil effects of Christian marriage; the state has authority to regulate the marriages of non-baptized subjects, since theirs is a purely natural contract.

*No authority over Christian marriage: Because it is a sacrament. The state has no power regarding Christian marriage itself, its essential properties, impediments, etc.*

*Has authority over civil effects of Christian marriage: The state may impose conditions to be observed, e.g., notification, registration, etc. The state has the right to legislate regarding dowry, succession, titles, property, etc., for the common good.*

*Authority to regulate marriage of non-baptized: But may not interfere with marriage as an institution, nor with its essential properties which are established by the natural law.*

QUESTION 132: **Can the state grant a divorce?**
ANSWER: It is beyond the power of the state to grant a divorce, even in the case of non-sacramental marriage between the unbaptized; the state, in legalizing divorce, violates the natural law and divine positive law.

*Divorce: A dissolution of the marriage bond, with the "right" to contract a new marriage.*

*Beyond power of state: It is God who joins husband and wife in the bond of marriage; only God can sever that bond. "What God hath joined together, let no man put asunder" (Mt. 19:6.)*

*Violates natural law: By natural law marriage is one and indissoluble by reason of its primary and secondary ends. (Q. 119.)*

*Violates divine positive law: "Whosoever shall put away his wife and marry another committeth adultery against her. And if the wife shall put away her husband, and be married to another, she committeth adultery." (Mk. 10:11-12.) The state in legalizing divorce legalizes adultery.*

QUESTION 133: **Has the Church any power to dissolve a marriage?**
ANSWER: The Church has no power to dissolve a true Christian marriage which has been consummated; but the Church has power to dissolve a true Christian marriage which is unconsummated in certain cases; she has also power to dissolve a true consummated marriage between unbaptized persons when the conditions of the "Pauline privilege" are verified.

*To dissolve: i.e., to sever the marriage bond and end its obligations.*

*Consummated marriage: A marriage is consummated when the marriage act has taken place and the parties are thereby made "one flesh".*

*Cannot dissolve a true, consummated Christian marriage: No power on earth, whether of man or of state or Church, can ever dissolve such a marriage.*

*Can dissolve a true, unconsummated Christian marriage: Such a marriage is a true sacramental union, but it falls short of its complete fullness, because unconsummated. The Church is the authentic interpreter of the meaning and extent of the divine law, and for adequate reasons, and under certain conditions, can dissolve such a marriage. The dissolution takes place by papal dispensation and by solemn religious profession.*

*Pauline Privilege (1 Cor. 7:10-17): A marriage between unbaptized persons is not a sacrament. If one of the parties becomes a Catholic, he or she is free to contract a sacramental marriage with a Catholic, by which the non-sacramental marriage (even if consummated) is at once dissolved. But the converted party must establish (a) that the other is unwilling to become a Catholic, and (b) is unwilling to live in peaceful wedlock with the Catholic spouse.*

QUESTION 134: **Does the Church sometimes grant a separation?**
ANSWER: The Church sometimes grants a separation (temporary or permanent) of husband and wife for grave reasons.
*A separation: But when the marriage is a true, Christian, consummated marriage this separation does not permit either party to marry again during the lifetime of the other.*
*For grave reasons: The Church is the judge as to whether the separation be temporary or permanent, and of the gravity of the reasons which justify separation.*

QUESTION 135: **Does not the Church sometimes grant a Decree of Nullity?**
ANSWER: The Church sometimes issues a Decree of Nullity, that is an official and authoritative declaration that a certain marriage, which seemed to be true or valid, was not really so.
*Decree of Nullity: Is not a dissolution of the marriage bond, but an official ruling that a particular marriage contract was null or void, because wanting in some essential necessary for a true marriage. Hence a Decree of Nullity is not an order declaring that the parties cease to be husband and wife, but an authoritative decision that they never were such before God.*

QUESTION 136: **What does the Church teach regarding the abuse of marriage called "birth control"?**
ANSWER: The Church condemns "birth control" or "birth prevention" as a grave abuse, and always a grave sin no matter what the motives or circumstances may be, because it is clearly a violation of the natural law and of divine positive law.
*Violation of natural law: Because it is the unnatural exercise of a faculty wherein the purpose for which the faculty exists is deliberately frustrated. Whatever name may be given to it, the act itself is nothing less than sexual perversion.*
*Violation of divine positive law: Forbidden by the sixth commandment.*
*No matter what the motives or circumstances may be, it is an evil thing in itself, like lying or suicide, and no motive or circumstance can ever justify it.*

*The act and habit of birth prevention springs not from alleged motives or hardship or health, but from an evil heart in which there is no love of God nor respect for his commandments.*

QUESTION 137: **Does the Church through her teaching on this question thereby forbid parents to limit the number of children, or compel them to have large families?**
ANSWER: The Church does not compel parents to have large families, nor does she forbid them to limit the number of children, but what she does forbid is the abuse of the marriage act and the sinful manner of artificial restriction.

*Church does not forbid limitation: But the only lawful way of restricting births is by the mutual agreement of parents not to exercise the marriage act and to observe continence (either always or at times). Those who say that this teaching of the Church is hard and difficult should remember the grace of the sacraments, which confers supernatural power to face the hardships and difficulties of the married state. To say that it is impossible to observe the laws of God is a heretical opinion, condemned by the Council of Trent.*

QUESTION 138: **Why is it that, even among Christians, there is not infrequently unhappiness in married life?**
ANSWER: Married persons are unhappy (a) because some enter marriage who are not called to it; (b) because many enter it from false motives; (c) because many only look at marriage from a purely natural standpoint, and ignore the spiritual; (d) because either party or both parties prove unfaithful to marriage vows;
(e) because they neglect the sacrament.

*Neglect of the sacrament: The sacrament of Matrimony confers on the contracting parties a right or title to supernatural help from God in all the problems and difficulties of married life. They must, however, pray and ask for these graces or helps. Many rely on their own natural powers and ability, and neglect the supernatural power which is at hand, to which they have a claim, and which God cannot refuse if they ask for it.*

QUESTION 139: **What does the Church teach regarding the right to marry and the obstacles to marriage?**
ANSWER: Since man has a natural right to marriage, and since it is necessary that the generality of men should marry (for the continuance of the race), the Church deplores and condemns undue restrictions on the part of individuals or of the state, as also the social conditions that

make it almost impossible for a very great number of men to marry.
*Church deplores: Because many are thereby needlessly exposed to grave temptation.*
*Church condemns undue restrictions: Which are prompted by the "gospel of comfort" and reluctance to give up the luxuries of single life and to undertake the responsibilities of married life. Nor should parents discourage their working daughters from marrying simply because they bring money to the home.*
*Social conditions: Principally the lack of a sufficient wage to marry.*

QUESTION 140: **What is the ideal of Christian marriage which the Church holds out to her children?**
ANSWER: The Church holds up to Christian youth the ideal of Christian marriage as a vocation to be worked for, a grave contract and a great sacrament, which requires Christian preparation and Christian judgment if it is to be happy, not only by nature but also by grace.
*Christian preparation: (a) Prayer and the sacraments, for guidance and help; (b) prudent advice, if necessary, from those best qualified to give it, e.g., parents or confessor; (c) calm reasoning, since it is a contract for life; (d) good use of time of betrothal and avoidance of sin.*
*Christian judgment: Keeping the spiritual aspect in view, and taking guidance from the teaching and law of the Church.*

QUESTION 141: **What is the dignity of Christian marriage, and how is it to be upheld?**
ANSWER: Since Christian marriage is a sacrament, and since even the marriage of pagans is a holy and sacred thing because instituted by God, it is sinful to make matrimony a subject of jokes, disrespect, or irreverence.
*Disrespect, irreverence: Films, plays, and novels which defend or condone matrimonial infidelity, divorce, or treat flippantly or suggestively of what is sacred in marriage, are agents of destruction in regard to marriage, and to morality itself, and should not be tolerated in a Christian community.*

THE RIGHT TO PRIVATE PROPERTY

CHAPTER 10
THE RIGHT TO PRIVATE PROPERTY

QUESTION 142: What is meant by the right to private property?
ANSWER: The right to private property is the right which a human being may have to use and dispose of material things for one's own benefit without interference.

*Private property: There is private ownership of things when they can be truly described as "mine", "yours", "theirs", etc.*

*To use and dispose: Therefore to "own" in the full sense of the word, so that one may consume, sell, give, exchange, or alter what is "his".*

*Material things: Animals or goods, but not a human being, because a human being is a person with a soul, having intellect and free will.*

*Without interference: Others have a duty to respect that right. There may not be interference with the lawful use or disposal of such things.*

QUESTION 143: Whence arises the right to private property?
ANSWER: The right to private property arises from natural law, and is sanctioned by divine law.

*Arises from natural law: Man has a duty to maintain life, imposed by natural law (Q. 76, 77), and that not only by his senses and physical powers (like animals), but by using his higher faculties of intellect and will. He is endowed with foresight, and can foresee what needs will arise in the future, and take steps to provide for them. To satisfy those needs, man requires material things, and not merely things that perish in the use (e.g., foodstuffs), but also those which can be used over again as the need arises (e.g., a plot of land). His intelligence urges him to seek after and acquire those goods and safeguard them against loss or deprivation. Therefore by natural law the right to private property is lawful and necessary. It becomes much more urgent and imperative considering man as head of a family depending on him for present and future needs.*

*Sanctioned by divine law: The seventh and tenth commandments enjoin respect for the right to private property as a strict and just right. The Church teaches that the right to private property does not arise from convention or agreement among men, but is given by nature itself. "To possess private property as one's own is a right given to man by nature"
(Leo XIII, Rerum Novarum).*

43

A CATHOLIC CATECHISM OF SOCIAL QUESTIONS

QUESTION 144: Is man's right to private property limited in any way?
ANSWER: The right to private property is not absolute, but relative, and is limited (1) by the nature and purpose of things, and (2) by the fact that man is not an isolated individual but a social being, having relations and obligations to others.
*Limited by nature and purpose of things: (a) Some things cannot be owned, e.g., daylight, air, the sea, etc.—they are by their nature superabundant; (b) man may not do absolutely what he likes with things. All things have a purpose, and to abuse them is to use them against nature, and is immoral.*
*Limited because man is a social being: Man is a social being, and may not live to himself alone (Questions 56, 68). His rights are limited by the claims and rights of society. He must use his gifts and goods not to the detriment of others, but as a help to them. (Hence the principle of taxation is entirely justified.)*

QUESTION 145: Can the right to private property be limited by the state?
ANSWER: The state may have the right (and a duty) to interfere with private ownership, but only when the common good requires it, and only with regard to what the public interest demands should be controlled or owned publicly and not privately.
*A right and duty to interfere: Regulation or control of private ownership may be necessary and sufficient. On the other hand, it may be necessary for the state or municipality to forbid private ownership of a particular thing, or take over (but always with just compensation) from private owners. The state has the right and the duty to impose limits to private ownership when and as far as the common good and general welfare demand it. But state control or ownership may not extend to such proportions as to amount to a practical denial of the right to private property.*

QUESTION 146: Could the state abolish all private property in the interest of the common good?
ANSWER: The state has no authority to abolish what is a natural right of man; such a step would not be in the interests of the common good, but against it.
*The state has no authority to abolish: When the state comes into existence it finds individuals and families already in possession of this right, and therefore may not abolish it. The state is bound to observe the natural law (Q. 57 & 59). The right to private property is conferred on man by the natural law (Q. 143), and therefore the state may not abolish it.*

## THE RIGHT TO PRIVATE PROPERTY

*Against the common good: Whatever is against the natural law or the law of man's nature (Q. 56) cannot be for the common good of men. But to abolish the right to private property is to go against the natural law, and therefore would be against the common good.*

QUESTION 147: **Did not Jesus Christ disapprove of personal wealth and possessions, and therefore of private property?**
ANSWER: Jesus Christ taught that wealth and possessions are an obstacle to the "perfect following" of himself, and are to be voluntarily renounced by those who voluntarily choose to serve God by the counsels of perfection.
*Voluntary poverty (Mt. 19:16, 22; Lk. 18:18, 3): Voluntary poverty is not a command, but a counsel of perfection to be voluntarily practiced by individuals for the love of God. Jesus Christ nowhere demands voluntary renunciation of the multitude.*

QUESTION 148: **Did Jesus Christ uphold man's right to private property?**
ANSWER: Jesus Christ upheld and approved of private ownership of material things as a natural right of man.
*Jesus Christ upheld and approved: His speech and doctrine imply that private ownership of things is a natural right sanctioned by divine law.*
*The commandments of the old law—"Thou shalt not steal," "Thou shalt not covet thy neighbor's house, nor anything that is his," etc.—were repeated and re-enforced by Jesus Christ (Mt. 19:18-19; Mk. 10:19; Rom. 13:9).*

QUESTION 149: **Has the Church always upheld the right to private property?**
ANSWER: While recommending voluntary poverty as a counsel of perfection, the Church has always asserted the justice and necessity of private property.
*Church has always asserted: Whenever that right has been questioned or denied.*
*The Church has asserted it against the Waldenses (12th century) and Anabaptists (16th century), and against modern Socialists and Communists.*
*Justice and necessity of private property: Encyclical Letters of Leo XIII: (Quod Apostolici Muneris, December 28, 1878; Rerum Novarum, May 15, 1891, Graves de communi, January 18, 1901). Pius X, (Fin dalla Prima, December 18, 1903). Pius XI, (Quadragesimo Anno, May 1931.*

QUESTION 150: **What is the doctrine of modern socialism (properly so-called) and Communism regarding private property?**
ANSWER: Both socialism (properly so-called) and communism deny that man has from nature a right to private ownership of productive goods. They maintain that such goods belong to the community, and that the state therefore alone possesses the ownership and management of all the means of production
and distribution.

*Productive goods: Those goods which can be used over and over again, and are therefore means of production, e.g., land, money, capital in various forms, plant and machinery, etc.*

*State alone possesses ownership: Therefore there is only one kind of legitimate ownership, i.e., public ownership. All men are simply employees of the state or municipality.*

QUESTION 151: **How is it that, if the right to private property is a natural right, so many men have been, and still are, agitators of socialism and communism?**
ANSWER: What has led more than anything else to the agitation in favor of socialism and communism is the manifold abuses of the system of private ownership.

*Manifold abuse: Widespread neglect of the duties attached to property, disregard of the welfare of those from whose labor wealth is partly derived, domination, oppression, etc. They assume that these evils spring inevitably from inequality of wealth and opportunity, hence they are led to demand the abolition of all private ownership.*

QUESTION 152: **Do the abuses of private ownership (of which socialists and communists complain) really exist?**
ANSWER: Yes, grave abuses exist. The Church recognizes the existence of these abuses, and condemns them no less strongly than socialists and communists.

*Grave abuses exist: The goods of the earth are meant by the creator to supply the needs of all men so that they may live as human beings. The goods of the earth, and control of them, have been allowed to concentrate into the hands of a small number of men (often by unjust and immoral means) to the destruction of the general welfare. This has resulted in the luxurious domination of the few and the destitution of the many—the great social problem.*

*Church condemns these abuses: Unceasingly from Leo XIII to the present Pontiff, Pius XI.*

QUESTION 153: **What are the factors which have contributed to the abuse of private property and given rise to the social problem?**
ANSWER: The chief factors which have contributed to the abuse of the system of private ownership are (1) the exclusion of religion and morality from all economic affairs, (2) immoral principles, (3) abuse of wealth, (4) lack of action by the state in the interests of the common good.

*Exclusion of religion and morality from economics: In theory and in practice it has held that the rights of owners are absolute, and cannot be restricted by law—divine or human.*

*Immoral principles: Greed, avarice, desire for easy gain and quick returns, which lead to dishonesty, particularly in industry and commerce.*

*Abuse of wealth: Unsocial use of money, luxury of the idle rich, neglect of the duties of wealth.*

*Lack of action by the state: In permitting immoral principles to operate without interference. The doctrine of individualism, which held that the state should not interfere in economic affairs, is condemned by the Church—Pius XI, Quadragesimo Anno, May 1931.*

QUESTION 154: **Can these abuses be remedied?**
ANSWER: The Church teaches that not only can these abuses be remedied, but they must be remedied without delay.

*Abuses must be remedied without delay: "Unless serious attempts be made with all energy and without delay to put them (i.e., reforms) into practice, let nobody persuade himself that peace and tranquility of human society can be effectively defended against the forces of revolution." (Pius XI, Quadragesimo Anno, May, 1931.)*

QUESTION 155: **What is the remedy advocated by socialists and communists?**
ANSWER: Socialists and communists advocate the taking over by the state of all ownership and management of substantially all the means of production and distribution, so that the government, national and local, would be the owner and manager of all land and factories, banks, stores, transport, etc. Individuals would have no power or control over the production and distribution of such things, but would receive their maintenance from the state in return for services rendered.

QUESTION 156: **What is the attitude of the Church towards the remedy advocated by socialism and communism?**

ANSWER: The Church rejects and condemns the remedy advocated by Socialism and Communism because it is against the natural law, and could not be put into operation without grave injustice and violation of natural and divine law.

*The Church rejects and condemns: What the Church condemns is socialism or communism in the strict and complete sense (i.e., as defined in Questions 150 and 155). Because a system is called by some "socialism", or a proposal is labeled by others "socialistic", it does not follow that such a system or proposal thereby comes under the condemnation of the Church.*

*Against the natural law: It would remove not only the abuses of private property, but destroy the right to private property itself. Hence it would be contrary to the natural rights of mankind.*

*Injustice and violation of natural and divine law: The remedy could not be introduced without robbery and confiscation, destruction of all order, and injury to the common welfare. It is no remedy to replace injustice by injustice.*

QUESTION 157: Has the Church a remedy, and what is it?
ANSWER: The Church has a remedy which she has continuously advocated—it is the removal of abuses and the solution of the social problem by reform of the system of private ownership, as it exists at present.

*Remedy of the Church is reform: The Church maintains that the evils at present existing are the result not of the right to private ownership, but of the misuse of that right. The Church lays down the guiding principles by which reform can and must be effected.*

QUESTION 158: What is the first step in the reform which the Church advocates?
ANSWER: The Church teaches that the first step in the reform of the present system of private property is a reform of the hearts of men who work the system.

*Reform of the hearts of men: There must be a return to the spirit of the Gospel—a return to Christian life, Christian ideals, and Christian conscience, i.e., there must be a Christianizing of man in all his relations with God and men. There can be no effective reform without religion. "No leader in public economy, no power of organization, will ever be able to bring social conditions to a peaceful solution unless first, in the very field of economics, there triumphs moral law based on God and conscience." (Pius XI, Caritate Christi Compulsi)*

QUESTION 159: In what particular manner is this reform to be put into practice?
ANSWER: This reform is to be brought about through the application by all men of Christian principles of social justice and social charity to all organized relationships—politics, civil life, professional transactions, commerce, and industry.

*Christian principles of social justice: Must replace the immoral principles (Q. 153) which have held sway throughout the whole economic system, particularly between capital and labor.*

*Christian principles of social charity: These are to be applied, especially with regard to the use of property or wealth, according to the teaching of Jesus Christ and of his Church.*

QUESTION 160: What does Jesus Christ teach regarding the duties of property and wealth?
ANSWER: Jesus Christ teaches that abundance a possessions or wealth may be fraught with grave danger and is very liable to be misused. He also makes it quite clear that wealth always brings with it increased duties and responsibilities.

*Wealth fraught with danger: It may give rise to self-satisfaction and a sense of independence of and disregard for God and fellow men. It may lead to forgetfulness of the meaning of life and life purpose. (Q. 22, 23 & 24.)*

*Liable to be misused: "It is easier for a camel to pass through the eye of a needle than for a rich man to enter the Kingdom of Heaven." (Matt 19:24.)*

*Wealth brings increased duties: Jesus Christ taught that man has not the absolute use and disposal of his wealth; he has only the stewardship of his goods, of which he must render an account to God, and upon which his eternal destiny depend. (Mt. 25:14, 30). The rich man in the Gospel is condemned, not for having riches ,but for neglecting the poor at his gate (Lk. 16:19-31).*

QUESTION 161: What is the teaching of the Church of the obligation of social charity, particularly with regard to the use of wealth?
ANSWER: The Church teaches that all wealth is stewardship; that man has a right in justice to what is necessary for present and future needs of himself and his dependants; that once these needs are provided for, there arises a grave obligation in charity to use his surplus wealth for the benefit of others, especially the poor; and, lastly, all abuse of property whether by rich or poor is condemned.

*Obligation in charity: There are many ways in which this obligation may be fulfilled, e.g., by gifts of money, by endowment, by increasing wages, by increasing opportunity for work and wages, etc. All abuse of property is condemned: All selfish and anti-social use of possessions is forbidden, not only the luxurious extravagance of the rich, but also the foolish spending of the poor.*

QUESTION 162: **What are the obligations of the state with regard to the necessary reform?**
ANSWER: The Church teaches that the state has a grave obligation to uphold the right to private property, to safeguard it by removing present and preventing future abuses, and to encourage a wider distribution of private property.

*To uphold the right to private Property: It is essential to the common good that individuals and families be able to exercise a right given to them by nature.*

*To safeguard: By legislation which will remove existing evils and prevent further abuse. It is the state principally which can and must effect these reforms. "When we speak of the reform of institutions it is principally the state we have in mind." (Pius XI, Quadragesimo Anno, May 1931)*

*To encourage wider distribution of private property: The state must adopt as its policy the increase of small owners, and encourage and assist a wider distribution of property.*

QUESTION 163: **What is the first step towards a just and equitable distribution of created goods?**
ANSWER: The first step towards a more equal distribution of private property is the recognition of the right of labor to a living wage.

*Right to a living wage: Propertyless wage earners must be given the opportunity of acquiring a certain moderate ownership of some kind of property or goods. The propertyless wage earners have no means of saving except from their wages, hence the Church insists in the first place on the right of the worker to a living wage.*

CHAPTER II

THE RIGHT TO A LIVING WAGE

QUESTION 164: **What is meant by the wage system?**
ANSWER: The wage system is that arrangement whereby men give their energy or labor, for which they receive in exchange payment in money or wages, and so are enabled to live.

# THE RIGHT TO A LIVING WAGE

QUESTION 165: How is the wage system maintained?
ANSWER: The wage system is maintained through the wage contract; that is, the worker and the employer agree and place themselves under a strict obligation, the former to give his strength and skill, the latter to give a return in value or wage, agreed upon.

QUESTION 166: Does the Church admit that the wage system is just?
ANSWER: The Church admits the wage system as being in itself just.
*Wage system is in itself just: The principles underlying it are just, e.g., the free agreement, the use of a man's services as distinct from his person, etc. Injustice, however, may arise in the working of the system.*

*The Church admits the system in itself: "Labor is not a thing to be ashamed of, if we lend our ear to right reason and Christian philosophy, but is an honorable calling, enabling a man to sustain his life in a way upright and creditable." (Leo XIII, Rerum Novarum.) "Those who hold that the wage contract is essentially unjust are certainly in error." (Pius XI, Quadragesimo Anno.)*

QUESTION 167: What does the Church teach regarding the morality of wage contracts?
ANSWER: The Church teaches that all wage contracts must conform to the fundamental principles of natural justice and human dignity.
*Natural justice: That is, the justice required by the natural law. A fair day's work demands a fair day's wage. Work may vary. Work that is more efficient, or requires educational preparation, or demands much skill, is entitled to a higher remuneration. The value of the work performed is to be estimated, not by the judgment of employers alone, nor by that of workers alone, but by the common judgment of men; that is, by unbiased representatives of both classes. In general, equal must be rendered for equal.*

*Human dignity: Man's labor may not be sold or bought or bargained for like any other commodity or article. "It is shameful and inhuman to treat men like chattels to make money by, or look upon them merely as so much muscle or physical strength." (Leo XIII, Rerum Novarum.)*

QUESTION 168: What does the Church insist on with regard to remuneration for labor?
ANSWER: The Church insists that all workers in return for their labors are entitled to a living wage.
*"All workers entitled to a living wage" (Leo XIII, Rerum Novarum and Pius XI, Quadragesimo Anno.)*

QUESTION 169: **What is meant by a living wage?**
ANSWER: By a living wage is meant a wage which will enable a well-conducted and thrifty workman to live in reasonable comfort.

*To live in reasonable comfort: Hence a living wage does not mean "just enough to keep alive on". "Wages ought not to be insufficient to support a frugal and well-behaved wage-earner." (Leo XIII, Rerum Novarum.) "Every effort must be made that fathers of families receive a wage sufficient to meet adequately normal domestic needs." (Pius XI, Quadragesimo Anno.) A living wage therefore means a wage sufficient to keep a man up to his standard of moderate comfort, or, in other words, a wage sufficient to support himself and his family in Christian decency. What size of family? An average family; that is, four or five children.*

QUESTION 170: **Why does the Church insist on the wage earner receiving a living wage?**
ANSWER: The Church insists on the worker receiving a living wage because his labor represents the only and necessary means whereby he is enabled to live.

*Labor the only and necessary means of life: Man has a right to live, and. a duty to preserve life (Q. 76 & 77). He has therefore a natural right to procure what is required in order to live; but the propertyless wage earner has no other means of procuring that save by the wages he earns in exchange for his labor. Hence the Church insists that the value of a man's labor must equal the cost of a man's living.*

*It must also be remembered that the responsibility for the rearing of his children falls upon the breadwinner (Q. 94) who furthermore has the duty of bringing them up in conditions of Christian decency and to supply their reasonable and frugal requirements— all of which is impossible unless he receives a living wage.*

QUESTION 171: **Since the worker is entitled to a living wage, on whom falls the duty of supplying that living wage?**
ANSWER: The duty of paying the living wage falls primarily on the employer—failing him, on the community itself.

*Primarily on the employer: The first charge on industry is the support of those engaged in it, and the first duty of an employer is the payment of a fair wage. Hence, if an industry can afford to pay a living wage, the employer is bound to pay it.*

*Failing the employer, on the community: The whole community has a moral duty so to order its economic system that industry will be able to support those engaged in it. This duty rests not merely on the government but on all members of the community. It is therefore the duty of the community to remove those evils (such as, for example, unscrupulous competition) which make it impossible for an employer to pay a living wage.*

QUESTION 172: What is there to compel an employer to pay a living wage if the industry can afford it?

ANSWER: When an industry can afford a living wage to the worker, the moral law of natural justice and the voice of Christian conscience should compel the employer to pay it. If he will not listen to that, then the trade organizations of workers may influence him; and, finally, the state, by legislation, may have to compel him, particularly when the workers are weak and unorganized and the employer remains obstinate in refusing.

QUESTION 173: If an industry or business (through no fault of employer) cannot bear the strain of paying a living wage, what is the employer bound to do?

ANSWER: (1) He is not bound to pay a wage which the business cannot afford.
(2) Neither is he bound to pay a full wage to workers in preference to allowing himself a moderate recompense for his own work.
(3) But, having taken moderate recompense to cover his needs and those of his family, he may not set aside any further profit until he has paid his workers the just minimum rate of the living wage.
(4) "Let employers and employed join in plans and efforts to overcome all difficulties and obstacles, and let them be aided in this wholesome endeavor by the wise measures of the public authority." (Pius XI, Quadragesimo Anno.)
(5) "In the last extreme, counsel must be taken whether the business can continue, or whether some other provision should be made for the workers." (Pius XI, Quadragesimo Anno.)

QUESTION 174: Does the Church admit that wages may vary and, if so, to what extent?

ANSWER: The Church teaches that wages may vary (Q. 167), and that men are free to agree with employers regarding wages, but there is a just minimum below which wages may not fall without injustice.
*A just minimum wage: "Let the working man and the employer make free agreements, and in particular let them agree freely as to wages; nevertheless, there underlies a dictate of natural justice more imperious and ancient than*

*any bargain between man and man, namely that wages ought not to be insufficient to support a frugal and well-behaved wage earner. If through necessity or fear of a worse evil the workman accepts harder conditions because an employer or contractor will afford him no better, he is made the victim of force and injustice.' (Leo XIII, Rerum Novarum.)*

QUESTION 175: **How is a just wage to be estimated?**
ANSWER: A just wage is to be estimated not by applying one single principle, but by considering many things, particularly (1) what is required for the support of the working man and his family; (2) the condition or state of the business or industry; and (3) the economic welfare of the whole community.

*What is required for support of worker and family: According to the normal level of decent living in the locality in which he resides.*

*The condition of the business: "It would be unjust to demand excessive wages which a business cannot pay without ruin...though if the business makes smaller profits on account of want of energy or enterprise, or from neglect of technical or economic progress, this is not a just reason for reducing the worker's wages." (Pius XI, Quadragesimo Anno.)*

*Economic welfare of the whole community: Wages have a social aspect. A rate of wages too low or too high causes unemployment, with its attendant evils. Union of effort and goodwill must endeavor to secure a scale of wages that will offer opportunities of work to the greatest possible number.*

QUESTION 176: **Are the employer's obligations completely satisfied by the payment of a just wage?**
ANSWER: No. Besides paying a just wage, the employer is bound to provide proper working conditions; namely, sufficient rest, decent hours, and sanitary conditions.

*Sufficient rest: (1) In order that the worker may attend to the main purpose of life—his spiritual welfare; and (2) that he may attend to bodily needs, and renew his strength. "Neither justice nor humanity permit the exaction of so much work that the soul becomes deadened by excessive labor and the body succumbs to exhaustion." (Leo XIII, Rerum Novarum.)*

*Decent hours: The hours of labor should depend on the nature of the work and on his strength. Labor which is extremely arduous (e.g., in mining industries) should be compensated by shorter hours. The season of the year and the age and sex of the worker must be taken into consideration.*

## THE RIGHT TO A LIVING WAGE

QUESTION 177: **Are there abuses in the wage system as it is worked at present?**
ANSWER: Undoubtedly. Many workers do not receive a living wage, not even the just minimum, and "sweating" is practiced in every shape and form.

*"Sweating" in every shape and form: "Sweating" may be described as taking advantage of the poorer and more helpless class of workers (because unorganized) and may take the form of:*
*(1) Excessive hours of work.*
*(2) Unsanitary conditions of work.*
*(3) Unreasonable taxing of the worker's strength.*
*(4) Paying less to women simply because they are women.*
*(5) All labor which is underpaid.*

QUESTION 178: **Who are responsible for "sweated" labor?**
ANSWER: The whole community must bear the responsibility for the manifest injustice of "sweated" labor in a people supposed to be Christian and civilized.

*Manifest injustice of "sweated" labor: All forms of "sweating" have this underlying injustice, namely that a fair wage is not paid for the labor given, and the conditions under which it is exacted. In practice it is nothing less than "oppression of the weak". It is "defrauding laborers of their wages"—a sin "crying to heaven for vengeance".*
*"To exercise pressure upon the indigent and the destitute for the sake of gain, and to gather one's profit out of the need of another, is condemned by all laws, human and divine." (Leo XIII, Rerum Novarum.)*
*The whole community responsible: The consumer, in his passionate quest for the cheapest goods, shares with the middleman, the tradesman, and an indifferent government responsibility for the evil of "sweated" labor. "If the business does not make enough money to pay the workman a just wage, either because it is overwhelmed with unjust burdens or because it is compelled to sell its products at an unjustly low price, those who thus injure it are guilty of grievous wrong, for it is they who deprive the workers of the just wage, and force them to accept terms which are unjust" (Pius XI, Quadragesimo Anno).*

QUESTION 179: **What is the remedy for the evil of "sweated" labor?**
ANSWER: The only adequate remedy for "sweated" labor is one which goes to the root of the evil—underpayment. The remedy, therefore, is the payment of a just wage.

*The only remedy—a just wage: The root cause of every form of "sweating" is that the labor is not remunerated according to its value. The only cure is the payment of at least a just minimum wage.*

*Workers who labor under a "sweating" system must combine if possible, and organize to secure fair treatment. If they cannot combine, then it is the duty of the state to step in and enforce just payment, particularly in the case of women and child workers. Trade Boards or some such equivalent should be established for all "sweated" trades to ensure fair wages, decent hours, and sanitary conditions.*

QUESTION 180: Does the Church approve of labor unions?

ANSWER: The Church approves of labor unions, and defends the right and necessity of the workers to organize to secure their welfare.

*The Church approves and defends:* "We may lay it down as a general and lasting law that working men's associations should be so organized and governed as to furnish the best and most suitable means for attaining what is aimed at; that is to say, for helping each individual member to better his conditions to the utmost in body, mind, and property." *(Leo XIII, Rerum Novarum.)*

*The right to organize:* This right, which for some time was denied and resisted by a section of the community, is now generally recognized, and will scarcely be called in question again.

*Necessity of organization:* As single individuals, the workers can do little or nothing. In an economic system in which conscience is silenced, and moral principles of justice are unheeded, labor unions are necessary because they are the only means left whereby the workers can secure fair conditions of work and wages.

QUESTION 181: Have workers a right to "strike"?

ANSWER: The Church teaches that workers have a natural right and a just right to "strike", but the use of that right must be lawful.

*A natural and just right to strike:* Men are free to give or withhold their labor. They are justified in withdrawing it when they suffer injustice or oppression in the conditions of their work.

*Use of right must be lawful:* Men have the right to strike, but the use of that right is not always lawful; many things have to be considered before a strike can be declared lawful.

QUESTION 182: When is a "strike" lawful?

ANSWER: The Church teaches that a "strike" can only lawfully be invoked when there is a grave and just cause, when there is hope of success, other satisfactory solutions having failed. It is also necessary that justice and charity be preserved, and the rights of the public duly respected, if the "strike" is to be lawfully invoked.

*Grave and just cause:* A strike is made for some demand. That demand must be reasonable. The advantage to be gained must be considered together with the loss and suffering to themselves, their employers, the industry, and the country generally.

*There must be hope of success:* There must be a chance of obtaining what is demanded. History shows that strikes do not always achieve their aim. Failure or even compromise may leave conditions for all concerned worse than before.

*Other solutions having failed:* The other available means for reaching a satisfactory solution must have been tried and have failed.

*Justice and charity must be preserved:* A just agreement may be still binding, and thus render a strike unlawful. A worker cannot violate an agreement which is still binding on him, if (a) it was freely entered upon; (b) is moreover just in all its clauses; (c) and has been faithfully fulfilled by the employer. If such an agreement still remains binding, it is unjust to break it, and unlawful to strike. The justice of a sympathetic strike (that is, bodies of workers, who have no grievance of their own, ceasing work in order to lend their moral support to others) must be judged in the light of this principle.

*Rights of the public duly respected:* A strike that violates the rights of the whole community cannot be lawful. Thus a general sympathetic strike, embracing most of the workers of the country, is almost impossible without violating the rights of the public.

QUESTION 183: **Does the Church recommend the use of strikes?**
ANSWER: The Church, while admitting that men have a natural right to strike, discourages the use of that right, and urges that disputes be settled by other means more natural and satisfactory from every point of view.

*Church discourages the use of strikes:* The strike is the weapon of industrial war. Like the wars of nations it may have its justification. But, just as nations should endeavor to settle their disputes by wiser and more prudent methods, so also strikes ought to be forestalled by other means less harmful and dangerous. The strike foments class war, and is not infrequently attended by violence, disorder, and damage to trade and to the common welfare.

*Other means more natural and satisfactory:* Such as, for example, by conciliation, by arbitration, or by Trade Board agreements. It is the duty of the state, in the interests of the common good, to interfere when other means fail to secure a fair settlement.

QUESTION 184: **Are the claims of social justice satisfied by the payment of a just wage?**
ANSWER: Not always. The Church advocates the modification of the wage system by some measure of profit sharing: that is, industry ought

to be so planned that the worker receives not merely a wage but a share of surplus or net profits.

*Some measure of profit sharing:* The Church does not state in detail what methods or measures are to be adopted. She is content to state the principle of profit sharing. It is evident, however, that co-operation, co-partnership (wherever possible), and "bonus" systems are all in keeping with the principle laid down by the Church.

*Surplus or net profits:* When all expenses have been paid (namely fair interest on capital invested, rent, charges for renewal of plant, wages, and salaries) what remains over is surplus or net profit.

QUESTION 185: **Why does the Church advise some form of profit sharing?**
ANSWER: The Church advises some form of profit sharing as necessary for a wider and just distribution of private property or ownership.

*Necessary for a wider and just distribution:* The Church teaches the necessity of removing the evils in the system of private ownership by effecting a wider distribution of private property (Q. 162 & 163).
God intended the earth and its wealth to minister to the needs of all. Wealth must be so distributed amongst the various individuals and classes of society that the common good of all be thereby promoted. By fair wages and by profit sharing the workers can save, increase their possessions, rise above the hand-to-mouth existence, and enjoy a nobler and fuller life that brings peace and contentment.

QUESTION 186: **What does the Church teach regarding the claims of capital to all the fruits of industry?**
ANSWER: The Church condemns the claims of capital to all the fruits of industry as unjust.

*Capital's claims to all the fruits of industry unjust:* "This sacred law (of social justice) is violated by an irresponsible wealthy class who, in the excess of their good fortune, deem it a just state of things that they should receive everything and the laborer nothing." (Pius XI, Quadragesimo Anno.)
A system cannot be for the common good which concentrates all wealth and power in the hands of a few, while it imposes on the working man "a yoke which is little better than that of slavery." (Leo XIII, Rerum Novarum.)

QUESTION 187: **What does the Church teach regarding the claims of labor to all the fruits of industry?**

ANSWER: The Church condemns as equally false and unjust the claims of labor to all the fruits of industry.

*Labor's claim to all the fruits of industry unjust:* "*The law of social justice is violated also by a propertyless wage earning class, who demand for themselves all the fruits of production.*" *(Pius XI, Quadragesimo Anno.)*

*The principle behind this claim (that all the products and profits are created by labor alone, and belong by every right to the working man) is also condemned as false and immoral.*

QUESTION 188: **What precisely does the Church teach regarding the respective rights of capital and labor in the matter of the product of industry?**

ANSWER: The Church teaches that product is the result of the efforts of capital and labor combined; both have a right to a just share of profits.

*Product results from combined capital and labor:* "*It is entirely false to ascribe the results of their combined efforts to either party alone, and it is flagrantly unjust that either should deny the efficacy of the other and seize all the product.*" *(Pius XI, Quadragesimo Anno.)*

*Both have a right to a just share:* "*By these principles of social justice one class is forbidden to exclude the other from a share in the proceeds*".

"*Each one must receive his due share, and the distribution of created goods must be brought into conformity with the demands of the common good and social justice.*" *(Pius XI, Quadragesimo Anno.)*

QUESTION 189: **What recommendation does the Church put forward for the organization of industry?**

ANSWER: The Church advocates the re-establishment of vocational groups or corporations or guilds, binding together owners, managers, workers, and all who are concerned in the same trade or profession.

*Vocational groups or corporations: The economic arid industrial system should be organized on the basis of function. There must be a return to the spirit which inspired and animated the craft guilds and trade guilds, namely that each live for all, and all for each. Such associations or corporations should be open to all, and should enjoy a measure of self-government. In the absence of such associations, virtually nothing exists between the individual and the state; thus it is that the state becomes overburdened with "an infinity of occupations" which it cannot fulfill.*

*Binding together; all concerned: Capital and labor are indispensable to each other.* "*Capital cannot do without labor, nor labor without capital.*" *(Leo XIII, Rerum Novarum.) Since the interests of both are identical, common sense as well as Christian principles demand that they combine for the benefit of each and the good of all.*

QUESTION 190: **What should be the aim of such an association?**
ANSWER: The aim of such associations or groups or corporations should be (1) to end class-war and establish Christian harmony among all classes, (2) to further the interests of the whole group, and (3) to promote the common good of the community.
*To end class-war and establish harmony: Class war is condemned by natural and divine law, particularly by the law of Christian charity. Harmony and combination must replace contention and strife. The root of class-antipathy and cause of class-war is selfishness, which Christianity strongly condemns.*
*To further the interests of the whole group: That is (1) to root out evils which have crept into industry and trade, such as unregulated production, excessive competition, extortion, domination, and abuse of power; (2) to apply Christian principles of justice and charity to all relations between individuals and various classes; (3) to further not only material interests, but to safeguard and promote the spiritual and moral well-being of all concerned.*
*To promote the common good of the community: This must be kept in view, because the aim of all industry and trade should be human welfare.*

CHAPTER 12

THE INDIVIDUAL: RIGHTS AND DUTIES

QUESTION 191: **Are all men equal?**
ANSWER: The Church, while recognizing a natural inequality among men, upholds the spiritual equality of all men as "brothers of one another" and sons of a common father who is in heaven.
*Natural inequality among men: Men are unlike in mental endowment and strength of body; they differ in aptitude and capability; they are unequal in attaining and retaining temporal possessions. There never has been, and never can be, purely human equality among men.*
*Spiritual equality of all men: All have the same spiritual worth, duty, and destiny. All men come from the hand of their creator; all men have been redeemed by Jesus Christ; all men will be judged and rewarded or punished by God according to the exact measure of their merits and of their demerits.*

## THE INDIVIDUAL: RIGHTS AND DUTIES

QUESTION 192: Have all men equal rights and duties?
ANSWER: Since all men have equally the same human nature, and are equal in their origin and in their destiny, all men are equal in the essential rights and duties that flow from these facts.
*The same human nature: All men are equally constituted, that is made up of body (material) and soul (spiritual, with powers of intellect and freewill). (Q. 16 & 17.)*
*Equal in origin and destiny: (Q. 191, 18, 23, & 46.)*
*Equal in essential rights and duties: They cannot be denied without denying the nature of man and his necessary relation to God.*

QUESTION 193: What are the essential rights of every individual?
ANSWER: The Church teaches that by natural law and by divine law every individual person has a right to life, a right to be reared and educated, a right to liberty, a right to work, a right to rest and recreation, a right to practice religion, and a right to follow conscience.
*A right to life: And all that is implied in that right, namely (1) the right to be born, (2) the right to preserve and defend that life, (3) the right to maintain that life at a human standard in the matter of food, clothing, and habitation. (See Chapter VII.)*
*A right to be reared and educated (see Chapter VIII.)*
*A right to liberty (Q. 194.)*
*A right to work (Q. 195.)*
*A right to rest and recreation (Q. 196.)*
*A right to practice religion (Q. 197.)*
*A right to follow conscience (Q. 198.)*

QUESTION 194: What does the Church teach regarding the right of the individual to the enjoyment of liberty?
ANSWER: The Church upholds the right of the individual to the enjoyment of liberty, in so far as this does not infringe on the equal rights of others.
*Right to liberty: This is essential for maintaining the dignity of human personality and for the self-development of the individual. All undue interference with the liberty of the individual by the state is condemned. That the individual exists for the state is a pagan ideal, and must be vigorously rejected.*

QUESTION 195: What is to be understood by the right to work?
ANSWER: The right to work does not mean that any particular employer, or even the state, is bound to find work for a man, unless under exceptional circumstances, as, for example, great distress; but it does mean that a man may not be prevented in seeking to exercise his powers so that he may secure his livelihood.

*Neither any particular employer nor the state is bound to find work for a man: But the community is responsible for its economic and industrial system being so ordered that, under normal conditions, all employable persons may find employment. In times of great distress, and particularly of widespread unemployment, the state as well as individual employers must take steps to remedy unemployment, and so remove also its attendant evils. This is demanded not only by the necessity of the individual worker but also by the necessity of the common welfare.*

QUESTION 196: Why does the Church insist on the right to rest and recreation?
ANSWER: The Church insists on the right to rest and recreation because they are essential in order that man may live a full and happy human life, and in particular that he may have opportunities of satisfying the claims of religion.

*The right to rest and recreation: This right is apt to be overlooked and disregarded in industrial centers. By divine precept man has a right to leisure. Human dignity demands it, and human welfare, which requires that man should work, requires also that he should have rest from work.*

*To satisfy the claims of religion: Since this life is a preparation for the eternal life of heaven, man needs leisure in order to attend to the claims of God and of his soul.*

QUESTION 197: What does the Church teach regarding the individual right to practice religion?
ANSWER: The Church teaches that the right to practice religion is supreme; no power, whether of individuals or of the state, may sever that primary and intimate relationship between the soul and God; therefore man may not be hindered or prevented in performing the duties of worship, love, and service of the Creator, to whom he owes all that he is and all that he has.

QUESTION 198: What does the Church teach regarding freedom of conscience; that is, the right to follow conscience?
ANSWER: The Church teaches that every man has a right to follow

conscience, and to deny him that right is condemned by natural and divine law as immoral and unjust.

*To deny the right to follow conscience is immoral and unjust: It is only by following his conscience, that man can perform virtuous actions, which are necessary for attaining his last end, and on which his eternal happiness depends.*

*The employer who refuses a man work (which means his livelihood) because of his religion, the landlord who refuses a dwelling to a family because of their religion, the state which refuses equal assistance in education because of religion—all are guilty of practical denials of man's right to follow his conscience.*

QUESTION 199: What are the most important duties of every individual?
ANSWER: The Church teaches that among the most important duties of men are the duty of religion and the duty of working.

QUESTION 200: What does the Church teach regarding the duty of working?
ANSWER: The Church teaches: (1) that work is obligatory on man by divine precept, (2) that it is necessary for self-development, and (3) that some form of work or service is a duty which every individual owes to society of which he is a member.

*By divine precept: Genesis 3:19.*

*Necessary for self-development: A definite and useful occupation is necessary for physical, moral, and spiritual well-being. Work as a duty gives man self-respect, and gives dignity to labor, however humble.*

*Some form of work or service is a social duty: Self-imposed idleness is a crime not only against the individual conscience but against society.*

QUESTION 201: What is meant by the duty of religion?
ANSWER: The duty of religion means that man must satisfy the claims of God, that is he must know, love, and serve God with his whole being. For this purpose man was made, and without religion man cannot attain his ultimate end, which is the happiness of heaven.

*Must know God: His existence, God's relation to creatures, as their beginning and end, and God's revealed word. This implies further that man seeks for the true religion and the true Church wherein he will find God's word, God's law, and God's life.*

*Must love God: God must be loved and preferred to all else, and creatures are to be loved for his sake.*

*Must serve God:* By observing his commands and counsels.
*With his whole being:* With body and soul, therefore, by bodily or external worship and prayer, as well as interior.

**QUESTION 202:** What are the consequences of neglect of the individual duty of religion?

ANSWER: Neglect of religion results in neglect of other duties, both of justice and charity, and leads to excesses which, apart from their harmful effect on the individual, are direct causes of social disorder and distress.

*Excesses:* Such as, for example, intemperance, impurity, inordinate craving after pleasure, greed, wastefulness, etc.

**QUESTION 203:** What does the Church teach regarding the use of strong drink?

ANSWER: The Church condemns excessive drinking, insists on moderation, and approves of total abstinence.

*Moderation:* The moderate use of strong drink is lawful. Absolute prohibition is an undue interference with the individual right to liberty. (Q. 194.) Since excessive drinking may become a social evil, the state is justified in controlling its manufacture, sale, and consumption in so far as the common good requires it.

**QUESTION 204:** What does the Church teach regarding betting and gambling?

ANSWER: The Church teaches that betting and gambling are lawful in themselves, but are very liable to abuse, so much so that they may become serious social evils.

*Lawful in themselves:* That is on certain conditions: (1) the money or equivalent which the person stakes must be his own and at his free disposal (thus money that is part of wages and which is needed for maintaining himself or his family may not be staked); (2) the act must be free; (3) there must be no fraud or undue advantage on either side.

*Very liable to abuse:* They become immoral when too much time is spent on them, also when too much money or money which cannot be afforded is spent on them. They often occasion other sins, e.g., exciting avarice, inducing trickery, and leading to squandering and theft.

*Serious social evils:* To forbid them altogether is to violate the individual right to liberty. (Q. 194.) Yet because they do lead to abuse, and assume the proportions of a social evil, the state is justified in restricting opportunities for indulging in them.

QUESTION 205: What does the Church teach regarding the purpose of leisure and the use of recreation?

ANSWER: The Church teaches that the purpose of leisure is not that men may give way to mere idleness, but to afford opportunities for cultivating their minds and bodies with pleasant social intercourse, games, etc. Recreation must be used properly, in a manner which is in keeping with human dignity, and all over-indulgence in the pursuit of pleasure is condemned.

*Over-indulgence is condemned: Pleasure must not be made the sole aim nor the principal aim of life. The Church disapproves of extravagance, both in the amount of time and in the amount of money which are lavished on amusement.*

QUESTION 206: What does the Church teach regarding the evil of impurity?

ANSWER: The Church teaches that all deliberate indulgence in impure actions, words, or thoughts is serious sin, which, apart from the fact that it deprives the sinner of heaven, is a direct cause of other social evils.

*Impure actions, words, thoughts: Divine law condemns every form of impurity. (Eph. 5: 3-5; Mt. 5:28.)*

*Cause of social evils: The state, therefore, must take action to prevent the manufacture, sale, or exhibition of anything and everything that is an incentive to vice. Though much may be effected by energetic action of the state, the most important remedy is that of the Church, which would have every individual realize his personal responsibility and the duty of self-control. She offers the sanctifying grace of the sacraments, by which the will is strengthened in resisting temptation.*

QUESTION 207: What is the all-important truth which every individual must keep in mind?

ANSWER: The all-important truth which every individual must keep in mind is that he must save his own soul; that this can only be done by the individual himself, by fulfilling the individual responsibilities and duties which God has placed upon him,
for which he will be judged, and for which he will be rewarded or punished.

*Can only be done by the individual: There are other necessary helps. Grace is essential, but the individual will must co-operate. The Church will assist him, but no man will be saved merely because he is a member of it. Good parents, good companions, may prove helpful, but no man will be saved merely because he has a good mother or friend. The individual must "work out" his own "salvation".*

CHAPTER 13
THE FAMILY AND THE HOME

QUESTION 208: **What is the position of the family as a society?**
ANSWER: The Church teaches that the family is by nature a primary and necessary society for mankind with essential rights and duties proper to itself.
*Primary society: The individual is born into the family, and only becomes a subject of the state through the family. The family precedes the state in idea as well as in fact; its rights and duties precede those of the state.*
*Necessary society: The family is absolutely necessary for the propagation of the race and for proper rearing of children.*
*Rights and duties proper to itself: Every human being has his individual rights and duties (chap XII), but has further responsibilities from his or her position as member of a family, amid the relations which nature itself sets up with other members that society.*

QUESTION 209: **What are the relative positions of members of the family?**
ANSWER: Human beings, as individuals, have spirit equality, but as members of the family they have equal positions and unequal rights and duties, both by natural law and divine law.
*As individuals spiritually equal: (Q. 191 & 192.)*
*As members of family—unequal: As members of the family they differ in order or rank. The father is the head; the wife, as wife, is subject to husband; children are subject to parents. This is the order which nature itself dictates and which the divine law approves and sanctions. (Fourth Commandment.)*

QUESTION 210: **By what means is the society of family maintained?**
ANSWER: The family is maintained by parental authority which comes from God and resides in the father as head of the family.
*Authority: i.e., the moral right and power to direct the conduct of others who are subjects.*
*Parental authority from God: "There is no power but from God" (Romans 13:1).*

THE FAMILY AND THE HOME

*Parental authority is not despotic, and must only be exercised in conformity with the natural and divine law. (For example, a father has no authority to make his child steal.)*

QUESTION 211: What is the end of the family as a society?
ANSWER: The end or purpose of the family as a society is identified with the purpose for which marriage exists, as instituted by God and sanctified by Jesus Christ.
*Purpose or end of marriage: (Q. 117 & 118.)*
*Sanctified by Jesus Christ: (Q. 122 & 123.)*

QUESTION 212: What follows from the fact that the family is the primary and essential society, with God-given authority and its own responsibilities?
ANSWER: It follows that all undue interference with parental authority or with responsibilities and rights and duties of parents is immoral and condemned by natural and divine law. Furthermore, all social reforms must be approved or rejected according as they promote or injure the well-being of the family.
*Undue interference immoral: The state may interfere when parents fail in their duty; but the state may not unduly interfere with family responsibilities nor rob parents of their rights. Although the state has the right and duty to assist families and does so in many ways (e.g., clinics, educational grants, public assistance, etc.), such help or assistance does not give any power to assume parents' responsibilities nor any right to set aside parental authority.*

QUESTION 213: What are the principal duties of the family?
ANSWER: The principal duties of the family embrace: (1) The mutual duties of husband and wife, namely, mutual love and help and conjugal fidelity; (2) the duties of parents to children—love, and care for their corporal and spiritual education; and (3) the duties of children—love, reverence, and obedience to parents.
*Mutual duties of husband and wife: Since by marriage they are made one, and since by Christian marriage their union is an image of the union of Christ and his Church (Ephes. 6:25; Col. 3:18; 1 Tim. 2:15) there should be perfect spiritual and temporal union between husband and wife.*
*Duties of parents: Arise from purpose of marriage. Love is to be shown by desiring and working for the welfare of children, and by warding off dangers to soul and body.*

*Corporal and spiritual education: (Q. 94–99.)*
*Duties of children: Love, reverence, and obedience: Because: (1) children owe their existence, after God, to their parents; (2) because of the dignity of parents; (3) because parents wield God's authority.*

QUESTION 214: **Is a proper home essential for the well-being of the family?**
ANSWER: The Church teaches that a home, in the true sense of the word, is essential to the family for the normal growth and development of family life.

*A home in the true sense of the word: A home is not merely the place where the family eats and sleeps, but it is the place in which the mother gladly stays and to which the father and family gladly return.*

*Normal growth and development: No house is a proper home unless it is suited to the Christian development of family life and the growth of domestic virtues.*

QUESTION 215: **What is required of the material dwelling in order that it may be a proper home?**
ANSWER: The family dwelling must be such that it can be made a home; that is, it must afford privacy for the family as a whole and for its individual members; it must also be sanitary, spacious, and have reasonable conveniences.

*Privacy: For the family as a whole; that is, from other individuals and families. There must be privacy within the home, for individuals, so that purity and modesty may be preserved.*

*Spacious: For reasons of health; also to afford opportunity for recreation, hobbies, etc.*

*Reasonable conveniences: So that too much time or labor is not spent on drudgery.*

QUESTION 216: **On whom falls the duty of providing a home for the family?**
ANSWER: The duty of providing a suitable home falls on the father, as head of the family; if the father is unable (through absence of living wage) to provide such a home, then the community itself is responsible, and must ensure that every family shall have a decent home.

*On the father, as head of the family: The father must provide for his family not merely shelter from wind and rain but a home with moderate comforts. Hence it is wrong for a father to spend on his own amusement or indulgence what should be devoted to maintaining a decent standard of home life.*

*The community is responsible: Therefore the community must use its resources to provide decent houses at moderate rents.*

QUESTION 217: **What are the principal evils which threaten the family at the present day?**
ANSWER: The principal evils which affect the family at the present time are: (a) divorce; (b) exclusion of religion from school and home; (c) lack of parental discipline; (d) disobedience and disrespect for parents; (e) undue state interference with parental authority.
*Divorce: (Q. 121 & 132). Divorce breaks up the family itself and deprives children of a parent's help and guidance.*
*Exclusion of religion: and with it the basis of morality. (Q. 98.)*
*Lack of parental discipline: Children are allowed to develop habits of sloth, pleasure-seeking, and extravagance. Parents are guilty in the matter of vigilance over their children and display an increasing indifference as to what their children witness, what they read, and the company they keep.*
*Undue state interference: It is the aim of genuine socialism to set aside the parental authority and claim all children as wards of the state.*

QUESTION 218: **What, briefly, is the ideal of the Christian family?**
ANSWER: The Christian family is that society wherein father and mother, with mutual goodwill and self-sacrifice, founded on natural love, elevated and strengthened by grace, work and pray together that they may save their own souls and rear their children to be dutiful and virtuous Christians and worthy citizens.
*Natural love elevated and strengthened by grace: Mutual affection supernaturalized by the sacrament. (Q. 122 & 123.)*
*Work and pray together: Matrimony is the state of life which they have chosen in which to work out their salvation.*
*To rear their children as dutiful Christians: Every child is a sacred trust, given to parents by God, to be brought up for God and destined for eternal happiness with God.*
*Worthy citizens: The good Christian, the good Catholic, is necessarily a good and worthy citizen. (Q. 114.)*

QUESTION 219: **Have Catholics a model or example of family life which they should imitate?**
ANSWER: Catholics have a model and exemplar of perfect family life in the Holy Family of Jesus, Mary, and Joseph.

*Holy Family:* St. Joseph, the head of that family, was a "just" man. Mary was the Immaculate Virgin Mother. The child was Jesus Christ, the Son of God, who is himself truth, justice, and love.

*Exemplar of perfect family life:* From St. Joseph every father may learn his duty of love and service, and contentment with labor and hardship. Every mother may see love and devotion consecrated and supernaturalized in her who was "full of grace".

In the Holy Child, every child may see the lesson of obedience in that being the Eternal Son of God, he submitted himself to the will of creatures.

## CHAPTER 14
## THE STATE

**QUESTION 220: What is the state?**

ANSWER: The state is the community of individuals and families united under a common authority and organized for the common welfare of all.

*Individuals and families united and organized:* Man is born into a family, and finds himself also incorporated into a community of families which is called the state. Man therefore, who possesses rights and duties as an individual human being and as a member of the family, acquires further rights and duties as a member of the larger community or society which forms the state.

**QUESTION 221: How does the state arise?**

ANSWER: The state arises from nature, and is therefore part of the design of God, the author of nature, and in this sense is a divine institution.

*Arises from nature: a divine institution:* God made man and implanted in his nature a tendency and need for association. Thus the family is necessary for the development and perfection of the individual. The state is necessary for the perfection of families.

Both the family and the state are societies that arise from man's nature; they are therefore part of the design of the author of man's nature, and willed by God in willing man's perfection not merely as an individual but as a social being.

**QUESTION 222: By what means is the state maintained?**

## THE STATE

ANSWER: The state is maintained by civil authority, which comes, not from the people, but from God.

*Civil authority: The right and the power which the state possesses to direct the conduct of its citizens, with the corresponding duty of obedience on their part. Without this authority the state could not achieve its end, which is the common good of all its members.*

*From God: "This authority, no less than society itself, has its source in nature, and has, consequently, God for its author. Hence it follows that all public power must proceed from God; for God alone is the true and supreme Lord of the world. Everything, without exception, must be subject to him, and must serve him, so that whosoever holds the right to govern holds it from one sole and single source, namely God, the Sovereign Ruler of all. 'There is no power but from God.' (Rom. 13:1.)" (Leo XIII, Immortale Dei, November 1, 1885.)*

QUESTION 223: Have the people no part in setting up the authority of the state?

ANSWER: The Church teaches that political authority is not created by the people, but to the people belongs the right to determine in what hands the authority (which comes from God) shall reside and how it shall be exercised.

*The right of the people: Men may choose what form of government they shall obey (monarchy, republic, etc.). The effect of the people's choice "is simply to mark out the ruler, not to give him authority to rule: it does not delegate the supreme power, but determines the person that shall wield it." (Leo XIII, Diuturnum illud.)*

QUESTION 224: What follows from the fact that civil authority comes from God?

ANSWER: It follows that the power that governs us is not that of our equals but of our superior; all duly constituted government (of whatever forms) wields God's authority within its proper limit, and has a just claim to our homage, love, and service.

*State wields God's authority over us: The state, then, claims our allegiance not as representing the collective will of the community, but as representing the divine authority. The motive and sanction of our obedience to the civil power is not "the will of the people", but "the will of God".*

QUESTION 225: What is the end or purpose of the state?

ANSWER: The end or purpose of the state is to secure the welfare of the people at large, or the common good.

*The common good: The individual must secure what he needs for his personal well-being; the father must secure what is necessary for the well-being of the family; the state must supply what the individual and the family cannot supply or cannot supply effectively. The state therefore exists for the general or common good of its members and families—the welfare of the greatest possible number in the largest possible measure. The state, while benefiting the whole community, must especially protect the rights of the workers and the poor and provide for and promote their interests, since these "have no resources of their own to fall back upon, and must chiefly depend upon the assistance of the state." (Leo XIII, Rerum Novarum.)*

QUESTION 226: How does the state promote the common good or welfare?
ANSWER: The state must secure the common good or welfare: (a) by preserving order and protecting the rights of its citizens from danger from within or without (b) by actively promoting the private initiative of individuals, families, and other groups.

*By preserving order and protecting rights: The first right and duty of the state is to preserve peace and order in the community and to secure to each and all their rights. Hence the state possesses the right and the duty to make civil laws, to administer them, and to enforce them. The state must protect its people not only against the incursions of nature, but also against invasion or molestation from without. Hence the state has the right and the duty of maintaining an adequate defense force.*

*Actively promoting: "The true aim of all social activity should be to help members of the social body, but never to destroy or absorb them. Directing, watching, stimulating, restraining, as circumstances suggest and necessity demands." (Pius XI, Quadragesimo Anno.)*

QUESTION 227: Has the state absolute or unlimited authority?
ANSWER: The state has not absolute or unlimited authority. Its authority only extends to what comes within its own proper sphere (i.e., the temporal sphere) in the attainment of its own proper end (i.e., the common good).

*No absolute or unlimited authority: State authority may not supersede nor absorb all other authority, nor set aside the natural and supernatural rights of men, which cannot be surrendered. Hence the authority of the state is limited: the state may not deprive men of their essential rights as human beings, as members of a family, or as children of God with a supernatural destiny.*
*Within its own sphere: The state's sphere of action is limited to the temporal well-being of its subjects. The limits of the state's authority were made more*

THE STATE

*clear when Jesus Christ established his Church, to whom he gave his own divine authority to secure the spiritual and eternal welfare of all men (Q. 6, 66, & 67). Whatever pertains to the spiritual and eternal welfare of men is under the authority of the Church. The state which interferes in such matters and opposes or sets aside the authority of the Church is trespassing, and since it is acting beyond its proper sphere its authority loses sanction. Since states are bound to respect each other's authority, still more are they bound to respect the authority of the Church in carrying out her divine mission.*

QUESTION 228: Is the state at liberty to make and enforce any kind of laws, just as it pleases?

ANSWER: The state has authority to make and enforce laws which are necessary and helpful in attaining its end, but its laws (civil law) must be in harmony with and unopposed to the already existing natural and divine positive law.

*Natural law: Is binding on all men whether as individuals or in communities (Q. 57). The state has no authority or power to change the natural law (Q. 59). Civil law therefore must recognize, harmonize with, and supplement the natural law.*

*Divine positive law: All men, both individually and collectively, are bound to observe the divine law as taught by Jesus Christ and his Church (Q. 10). Hence the laws of the state may not render that duty difficult, much less impossible. God cannot give to a state the authority to contradict and oppose the authority of his Church (Q. 6).*

QUESTION 229: May the state interfere with the free actions and conduct of its subjects?

ANSWER: The state has the right and the duty to intervene or interfere in the conduct and actions of its subjects when the common good requires it; the state may be obliged to restrict the freedom of individuals when that freedom would be used to injure the rights of others and interfere with the general good; but the state may not interfere in those rights which are essential and fundamental to human nature.

*The right to intervene: Will vary with circumstances. To decide when interference is desirable or necessary requires good statesmanship.*

*Rights essential and fundamental to human nature: As, for example, the right to live, the right to marry, the right to rear a family, etc. (See Q. 193.)*

73

QUESTION 230: **What are the chief dangers to which the state is exposed?**
ANSWER: The two chief dangers to which the state is exposed are excessive interference and insufficient interference with human conduct in its relation to the common good.

QUESTION 231: **What of excessive interference? Are there any examples of it?**
ANSWER: Excessive interference arises from a false notion of the authority and function of the state, and is easily recognized in many instances.

*Arises from false notion of state:* Some regard the state as a huge impersonal being, distinct from and above all, which by its enormous powers and resources can subvert everything and everybody to its own will and its own enrichment. The truth is that the state exists and holds its authority (from God) in order to supplement the efforts of the individuals and the families forming the state. The state is the servant rather than the lord of all. That the individual exists only for the state, and not the state for the individuals, is a pagan theory, and must be rejected.

*Excessive interference—examples:*

*(1) Interference with the institution and essential properties of marriage as established by natural law. Divorce (Q. 131 & 132).*

*(2) Interference with Christian marriage, which is a sacrament and is under the authority of the Church, legalizing divorce or dissolution of Christian marriage (Q. 124–126 & 131).*

*(3) State sterilization of defectives and others (Q. 91).*

*(4) Excluding religion from education, making it practically atheistic (Q. 103–107).*

*(5) Undue interference with parental authority (Q. 210).*

*(6) In certain countries interfering with the essential rights of the individual (Q. 193).*

QUESTION 232: **What of insufficient interference?**
ANSWER: Insufficient interference on the part of the state is the result of the false view that the state should not interfere with the private dealings and business of its subjects. There are many instances where the common good demands state intervention and where the state does nothing.

*False view:* It originated after the Reformation and was upheld by a

*certain school of economists. Such teaching is condemned by the Church: "Whenever the general interest or any particular class suffers, or is threatened with mischief which can in no other way be met or prevented, the public authority must step in to deal with it." (Leo XIII, Rerum Novarum.)*
*Many instances:*
*(1) Not seeking to remedy the evils and the injustice which foment class war and cause strikes (Q. 162 & 153).*
*(2) Not checking the manifest injustice of "sweating" in every shape and form (Questions 177–179).*
*(3) Not promoting a wider distribution of property.*
*(4) Not checking unscrupulous competition.*
*(5) Not protecting the weak against the domination and oppression of the fortunate few in the matter of agriculture and in industry and trade.*

QUESTION 233: Have states rights and duties to each other?
ANSWER: States, like individuals, are subject to the natural law and divine law, hence they are bound to observe justice and charity to each other.
*States subject to natural and divine law: (Q. 10 & 57.)*
*Justice: Each state must respect the just rights of other states, and endeavor to observe peace with others. War may be necessary and justifiable when all other means of settling disputes have been tried and failed, but war is contrary to the Christian ideal. Wars are caused by putting national interests before the law of God, by false and inordinate ambition, by unbounded commercial greed, by fostering of racial and religious hatreds, by the immoral projects of selfish rulers and statesmen. War shall end, and peace reign, only when governments accept and act according to Christian principles. This will not come about until the people who form the state are educated to be true Christians individually, socially, and internationally.*
*Charity: The state has duties of charity in assisting another in distress, or upholding by protest and sometimes by force the cause of oppressed weak nations.*

QUESTION 234: Did Jesus Christ give any guidance to his followers in the matter of civic duties?
ANSWER: Jesus Christ gave his followers definite guidance on their civic duties when he said "Render to Caesar the things that are Caesar's, and to God the things that are God's." (Mt. 22:21; Lk. 20:25.)
*The things that are Caesar's: Jesus Christ proclaimed Caesar's right to obedience and tribute not as an independent authority nor as a rival authority but as representing in purely earthly affairs the Lord and Master of all. Christ himself professed respect for Pilate for the power given him from*

*above (Jn. 19:2). Therefore the Christian must obey and respect civil authority.*

*The things that are God's: In the things that pertain to God we must render to God, and obey God rather than men. Hence if civil law should attempt to violate divine law we must reject it. The first of all man's relations and duties are those between his soul and God—nothing may interfere with or destroy that relationship. God's service must come even before that of the state. No power may take from man the right to know God and to follow conscience in his service.*

*The words of Jesus Christ contain the basis of the constitution of Christian states, and while they point out the necessity of civil obedience they at the same time establish the act of freedom for all men.*

CHAPTER 15
THE CATHOLIC AND POLITICS

QUESTION 235: **Are Catholics free to take part in politics?**
ANSWER: Catholics are free to take part in politics; moreover it is their duty to interest themselves in the affairs of the community.

*Politics: Matters relating to systems of government and administration of what concerns public welfare.*

*Duty to take interest in affairs of community: (a) Because every individual is a social being with social obligations and duties to fellow citizens and to the state; (b) Because adults have the responsibility of the vote, which must be exercised according to an enlightened conscience; hence every adult must interest himself in the affairs of his country both in its internal government and in its external relations with other states.*

QUESTION 236: **May a Catholic be a member of a political party?**
ANSWER: A Catholic may be a member of a political party provided the party does not definitely take its stand on non-Christian principles.

*Non-Christian Principles: The party must not have a non-Christian basis or constitution. This is a necessary condition. Fortunately the three principal parties in this country (i.e., Conservative, Liberal, and Labor) satisfy this condition; hence a Catholic may be a member of any one of them.*

THE CATHOLIC AND POLITICS

QUESTION 237: May a Catholic give his support and allegiance to his party in its entire program?
ANSWER: No. A Catholic may only give support and allegiance to his party in so far as its proposals are in keeping with Christian principles.
*As far as it is in keeping with Christian principles: None of the parties (Q. 236) has a program which is entirely in accord with Christian principles. The Catholic may only give his allegiance with certain limitations. Each party is influenced by outside affiliations and agencies that affect and may even dictate its policy, sometimes in defiance of natural and divine law. A Catholic must exercise the right to differ from, and even oppose, his party when it advocates measures that violate the natural and divine law. On questions of morality the Catholic must take his guidance, not from a political party, but from the teaching of the Church, divinely instituted for this purpose, and infallible. In the event of conflict between the Catholic's conscience and the demands of his political party he must obey his Catholic conscience and withstand the demands of his party. "We must obey God, rather than men." (Acts 5:29.)*

QUESTION 238: May a Catholic be a socialist or a communist?
ANSWER: No Catholic can be a socialist or communist in the strict sense of the word, without ceasing to be a Catholic.
*A socialist or communist in the strict sense: A socialist or communist in the strict sense of the word is one who identifies himself with the socialist creed and principles regarding man's nature, origin, and destiny, and the functions of the family and the state.*
*No Catholic can be such: "No one can be at the same time a sincere Catholic and a socialist properly so-called." (Pius XI, Quadragesimo Anno.) The basic principles of socialism and communism in the strict sense of the word are condemned by the Church. No Catholic can accept them and remain a Catholic.*

QUESTION 239: Does the Church condemn communism (and strict socialism) solely because it denies the right to private property and preaches class war?
ANSWER: The Church condemns communism (and strict socialism) not merely because it denies private property and urges class war, but also because of its teaching in theory and practice regarding God, religion, morality, marriage, education, and many other truths.
*God-Communist theory: There is no God. Communist practice: "The masses of the world must be provided with every kind of atheist propaganda" (Lenin, March, 1922). "We will grapple with God, we will conquer him in*

77

*the highest heaven; and wherever he seeks refuge we will subdue him forever" (Zinoviev, December, 1923).*
*Religion-Communist theory: All religion is false—opium for the people. Communist practice: "We must declare war on all forms of religion" (Pravda. April 13th, 1928).*
*Morality-Communist theory: There is no moral law and no fixed standard of morality. Communist practice: "For communists morality consists entirely in class war" (Lenin). "The school must explain the falsehood of morality" (Lounatcharsky, March 26th, 1929).*
*Marriage-Communist theory: Marriage is not a stable legalized union of man and woman. Communist practice: "Divorce is easy at any moment at the will of either party. The distinction between legitimate and illegitimate children has been abolished" (Soviet Marriage Code).*
*Education-Communist theory: Parents have no right to educate their children. This right belongs to the state. Communist practice: "The teaching of religion in either public or private schools is prohibited under penalty of penal servitude" (Clause 121, Soviet Code). "We must remove children from the baneful influence of the family" (Madame Lelina, Director of Education in Leningrad). "Immorality in the schools is making satisfactory progress" (Madame Kollontai, 1922). "Where the new proletarian school is established, the boys and girls are taught that everything is allowed" (Pravda, March, 1925).*

QUESTION 240: **What is the aim of the Church's social teaching?**
ANSWER: The aim of the Church's social teaching is not to support one political party against another, nor to establish a rival political party, but to ensure that all men, both those who are governed and those who govern, recognize their Christian principles to their individual, civic, and political activities.
*Aim of Church's social teaching: "To make the conditions of those who toil more tolerable; to enable them to obtain, little by little, those means by which they may provide for the future; to help them to practice in public and in private the duties which morality and religion inculcate; to aid them to feel that they are not animals but men, not heathens but Christians, and so enable them to strive more zealously and eagerly for the one thing which is necessary: the ultimate good for which we are all born into the world" (Leo XIII, Graves de Communi).*

QUESTION 241: **Will the remedies and reforms put forward by the Church solve all social problems?**

ANSWER: The Church does not claim that her social teaching will turn the world into an earthly paradise, but she does claim that her teaching, if accepted by men, will solve all social problems to a certain degree.

*No earthly paradise: We must beware of all who promise for their schemes an era of unalloyed happiness. The Church does not claim that her social teaching, even if accepted by the world, will achieve the impossible. Perfect happiness is to be obtained only in the next life. This world, this present life, is necessarily a testing and a proving of man's worthiness.*

*Will solve to a certain degree: The reforms of the Church are aimed at removing the serious evils which underlie these problems, and at improving the conditions of life and labor. If accepted by men, they will restore justice and charity to working conditions and relations; they will make the lives of the vast majority of men more in keeping with their dignity as men and more pleasing to God.*

QUESTION 242: **What is the first duty of a Catholic in the midst of social problems?**
ANSWER: The first duty of a Catholic is to inform himself of the Church's authoritative teaching on social questions.

*First duty: Catholics may not remain indifferent when Christian morality and social justice are in danger or are actually violated. Ignorance cannot be excused in the case of Catholics who hold positions of importance on administrative bodies. Still more weighty is the duty of the clergy "No easy task is here imposed upon the clergy: wherefore all candidates for the sacred priesthood must be adequately prepared to meet it by intense study of social matters" (Pius XI, Quadragesimo Anno).*

QUESTION 243: **What is the next duty of the Catholic?**
ANSWER: Having learned what the Church teaches, the Catholic must accept the teaching of Christ and his Church as his guide.

*The Catholic must accept: "He that is not with me is against me" (Lk. 11:23).*

QUESTION 244: **Is it sufficient for the Catholic to know and accept the teaching of the Church on social questions?**
ANSWER: It is not sufficient for the Catholic to know and accept the teaching of the Church on social questions; he must put it into practice, and he must begin by applying it to his own life.

*Put it into practice: "Faith without works is dead" (James 2:20). The individual must be a Catholic in thought, word, and action. To call oneself a Catholic, and even to accept the Church's teaching, without putting it into practice merits the condemnation which Jesus Christ passed upon the*

*Pharisees, who "say, but do not" (Mt. 23:3; Lk. 11:52).*
*Begin with his own life: The Catholic must apply the Church's teaching to his own life, his home, his profession, or business or work. One cannot hope to change the face of the earth without first changing one's own heart.*

QUESTION 245: **Has a Catholic any duty beyond regulating his own individual life?**
ANSWER: The Catholic has a further duty of laboring to restore society in all its activities and institutions to the Christian ideal.
*In all activities and institutions: Godless government and Godless politics lead inevitably to selfish individualism and state tyranny. Parliaments, local governments, boards of administration and control, etc., must be made to recognize the law of God as supreme. Only by recognizing God and accepting his laws as supreme will states as well as individuals prosper. "Seek first the Kingdom of God and his justice and all these things will be added unto you" (Mt. 6:33).*

QUESTION 246: **What are Catholics to do in a country whose people no longer recognize the law of God as supreme, and who have, to a large extent, abandoned Christian ideals?**
ANSWER: It is the duty of Catholics not to sit idle or remain indifferent; but by word and example, and by united effort, they must endeavor to correct the evils of our social system and restore it to Christian order, peace, and prosperity.
*By word: Catholics must enlighten public opinion. They must point out what is wrong and how it is to be remedied. They are better equipped than others for the task since they have the true principles of Christ and his Church to guide them.*
*By example: We must apply our belief to our conduct, recognizing that we are the "light of the world", "salt of the earth", and the "leaven" which is to ferment the whole.*
*By united effort: There must be union of wills and effort among Catholics, particularly in the exercise of those rights which belong to them as citizens.*

QUESTION 247: **What is the surest hope for Christian reconstruction of the social order, and for the preservation of Christian civilization?**
ANSWER: The surest hope for Christian reconstruction of the

social order and for the preservation of Christian civilization is the return of all to the one true Church, established by Jesus Christ to teach men and guide men infallibly through earthly life to the eternal happiness for which they are all created.

*The one true Church: The Catholic Church alone speaks with God's authority. She alone is uncompromising in her teaching; she will not change eternal truth or law at the request of mortal men. She alone is unerring in her guidance, since Jesus Christ has promised to be with her "all days, even to the consummation of the world" (Mt. 28:20).*

*Within her teaching and under her guidance there is light, order, true freedom, and true happiness; outside is error, disorder, slavery, and the darkness of despair.*

# OTHER TITLES AVAILABLE ON CATHOLIC SOCIAL QUESTIONS

Beyond Capitalism and Socialism - Anthology - HB $21.95
Action - Jean Ousset - PB $17.95
Catholicism, Protestantism, and Capitalism - Fanfani - PB $16.95
The Church and the Land - Fr. Vincent McNabb - PB $16.95
The Death of Christian Culture - John Senior - PB $23.95
Distributist Perspectives - Volume 1 - PB $10.95
Distributist Perspectives - Volume 2 - PB $12.95
Dollfuss - An Austrian Patriot - Fr. J. Messner - PB $14.95
Economics for Helen - Hilaire Belloc - PB $14.95
An Essay on the Economic Effects of the Reformation - PB $14.95
Essay on the Restoration of Property - Hilaire Belloc - PB $11.95
Ethics & the National Economy - Heinrich Pesch, S.J. - PB $15.95
Flee To The Fields: Anthology - PB $14.95
The Free Press - Hilaire Belloc - PB $10.95
The Gauntlet - Arthur Penty - PB $10.95
The Guild State - G.R. Stirling Taylor - PB $13.95
Irish Impressions - G.K. Chesterton - PB $14.95
Miscellany of Men - G.K. Chesterton - PB $15.95
Nazareth or Social Chaos - Fr. Vincent McNabb - PB $12.95
Outline of Sanity - Chesterton - PB $16.95
The Party System - Belloc/Chesterton - PB $14.95
Restoration of Christian Culture - John Senior - PB $21.95
The Rural Solution - PB $11.95
The Church at the Turning Points of History - Kurth - PB $14.95
Utopia of Usurers - Chesterton - PB $13.95
The Tragedy of James Connolly - Fr. Denis Fahey - SmB $6.95
The Rulers of Russia - Fr. Fahey - SmB $7.95
The Rulers of Russia & the Russian Farmers - Fr. Fahey - SmB $7.95
Money Manipulation and Social Order - Fr. Fahey - SmB $7.95
Workingman's Guilds of the Middle Ages - Godefroid Kurth - $6.95